# UNSPEAKABLE

# UNSPEAKABLE

## CHRIS HEDGES
### on the Most Forbidden
### Topics in America

### with DAVID TALBOT

Hot Books

Hot Books books may be purchased in bulk at special discounts for sales promotion, corporate gifts, fund-raising, or educational purposes. Special editions can also be created to specifications. For details, contact the Special Sales Department, Skyhorse Publishing, 307 West 36th Street, 11th Floor, New York, NY 10018 or info@ skyhorsepublishing.com.

Hot Books® and Skyhorse Publishing® are registered trademarks of Skyhorse Publishing, Inc.®, a Delaware corporation.

Visit our website at www.hotbookspress.com

10 9 8 7 6 5 4 3 2

Library of Congress Cataloging-in-Publication Data is available on file.

Cover design by Brian Peterson

Print ISBN: 978-1-5107-1273-7
Ebook ISBN: 978-1-5107-1274-4

Printed in the United States of America

# Contents

# Introduction

By David Talbot

Our media has become such an all-encompassing echo chamber of power—or its corollary, a bright and shiny distraction from our misery—that it's a shock whenever a dissident voice breaks through this wall of sound. One of the most singular and bracing voices of dissent in our time belongs to Chris Hedges. He is no stranger to the corporate ranks of journalism, toiling for over two decades as a war correspondent, primarily for the *New York Times*, where he shared a Pulitzer Prize for team reporting on the events of 9/11. But even as a *Times* man, Hedges clearly stood out from the press pack. His fearless reporting from Central America (before he joined the *Times*), and later from the Middle East, Africa and the Balkans, routinely contradicted the official line, evoking the rigorous independence of his literary heroes, George Orwell and James Baldwin. Like Orwell and Baldwin, Hedges has consistently refused to toe party lines or trim his reporting to fit conventional patterns.

He inevitably developed a reputation for being "abrasive" at the *Times*, and after he reaffirmed his independence of mind by speaking out against George W. Bush's invasion of Iraq at the commencement ceremony of a—until then –placid Midwestern campus, life at the newspaper of record became untenable for Hedges, who struck out on his own.

Life as an independent thinker and writer has presented a different set of challenges. It is not easy to support oneself, much less a family, as a public intellectual without the benefits of a university teaching position or think-tank sinecure or the rainbow of corporate endowments that grace the lives of the dutiful courtiers who dominate our national discourse. Hedges lives in Princeton, New Jersey, but he is not on the faculty at Princeton (although he has had two visiting professorships at the university). He teaches, rather, college credit courses in a maximum security prison. Still, he has managed to make a living through the power of his writing and speaking—and although his books are customarily slighted and impugned by his former newspaper, they have attracted a large and loyal following and have succeeded in shouldering their way onto the *New York Times* Bestseller List.

Among his significant titles are *War Is a Force that Gives Us Meaning*, a provocative reflection on the gods of fire and death that rule our lives (including, for two decades, Hedges'); and *American Fascists: The Christian Right and the War on America; Death of the Liberal Class*; and *Wages of Rebellion: The Moral Imperative of Revolt*—books filled with alarming insights into the devolution of American society and politics and radical calls for action, even against seemingly invincible odds.

Hedges, who has put his writing and speaking skills at the services of the Occupy movement and many other apparently quixotic crusades for social justice, calls this indomitable will to resist "the sublime madness of the soul," quoting the theologian Reinhold Niebuhr. "Perhaps in our lifetimes we will not succeed," Hedges has written. "Perhaps things will only get worse. But this does not invalidate our efforts. Rebellion – which is different from revolution because it is perpetual alienation from power rather than the replacement of one power system with another—should be our natural state."

Hedges, who is the son of a Presbyterian minister and a graduate of the Harvard Divinity School, has the temperament of a biblical prophet as he rails against the evils of the capitalist system, US imperialism and racism—and the brutal treatment of those whom our ruling powers have turned into what Noam Chomsky calls "the unpeople," including Palestinians, immigrants, prisoners and the poor. His friend, Stephen Kinzer, once told Hedges: "You're not a journalist. You're a minister pretending to be journalist." And there is some truth to that, concedes Hedges. The columns he writes for publications such as *Truthdig*—and collected in volumes like *The World As It Is*—do read like sermons. But these are not the sermons of a kindly and serene suburban minister—they are meant to stir unease and trouble. "Sermons, when they are good, do not please a congregation," he writes. "They do not make people happy. They are not a form of entertainment. They disturb many, if not most, of the listeners. They resonate only with a minority…Sermons force those who hear them to be self-critical."

Hedges is particularly committed to disturbing the tranquility of the powerful. He is proud of the fact that he never was considered a member of the elite media club. "My former employer, the *New York Times*, with some of the most able and talented journalists and editors in the country, not only propagated the lies used to justify the war in Iraq, but also never saw the financial meltdown coming," he writes in the introduction to *The World As It Is*. "These journalists and editors are besotted with their access to the powerful. They look at themselves as players, part of the inside elite. They went to the same elite colleges. They eat at the same restaurants. They go to the same parties and dinners. They live in the same exclusive neighborhoods. Their children go to the same schools… The media treat criminals on Wall Street as responsible members of the ruling class. They treat the criminals in the White House and the Pentagon as statesmen… The media are hated for a reason. They deserve to be hated. The few journalists who do not function as entertainers and celebrities are so timid and removed from the suffering of our dispossessed working classes that they are rightly despised."

Because he stands in contemptuous opposition to the media establishment, Hedges has been marginalized. He does not get invited to comment on the major issues of the day by the cable news networks or even by public television or National Public Radio, which were intended to give space to a diversity of voices. He will never be given a prestigious platform to comment on the crimes of Wall Street and our permanent war machine, or the criminalization of poverty and the legal immunity of the privileged, or the corporate and political exploitation of women's bodies, or the crying need for a radical transformation of our society. But Hedges does talk about all this and much more in the following pages.

He says that it does not trouble him being sidelined by the corporate media. "If you measure your success by your impact…then you will easily be seduced into re-configuring what you do," Hedges told me in the course of our lengthy conversation. "Obviously, I want to have an impact. But I don't want to cater to the wider culture. I won't speak in ways that they dictate. At that point I become like them…You have to hold fast to your integrity. I am shut out for a reason."

But if his marginalization doesn't bother Hedges, it should bother us. His insights and opinions—which have been hard-earned over a tumultuous career of covering war and revolution, suffering and liberation—should be part of our national debate.

This is why we are launching the "Unspeakable" series at Hot Books/Skyhorse, to provide another venue for people like Hedges—those essential thinkers, writers and activists who have been kept carefully away from the media spotlight.

I spoke with Hedges over a marathon, six-hours stretch on a chilly March day in Princeton, huddling over cups of tea and salads and sandwiches at a vegetarian restaurant and then at a nearby tavern. In the following weeks, we kept the conversation going through email. Since we're both writers, we polished some of our questions and answers during the editing process, for clarity and precision.

The conversation with Chris Hedges is the first in the "Unspeakable" series. We hope to lift the political conversation in America from the imbecilic and benighted depths to which it has sunk. We believe the public is ready for a discourse that assumes their intelligence and whets their appetite for taboo ideas. We all want to understand not only how we got into our current abysmal predicament, but how we might crawl out.

Our body politic has grown sluggish and dull-witted, stuffed with a steady diet of junk media and corporate propaganda. It's time to light a fire under this slumbering giant, American democracy. It's time to think dangerous thoughts. Welcome to Hot Books…and our "Unspeakable" series.

# I. The Making of a Radical

**What made you a radical?**

It's a combination of factors—including my personality type. I grew up in a literate household, in a farm town of 2,000 people in upstate New York called Schoharie. My mother, when I was a kid, was a teacher and ended up becoming an English professor. My father was a World War II army veteran—he had been a cryptographer in the North Africa, Palestine and Iran—and a Presbyterian minister. They were very involved in the 1960s in the civil rights movement and the anti-war movement. My dad took my younger sister and me to protests.

Dr. Martin Luther King, especially in rural white enclaves, was at the time one of the most hated men in America. Standing up for racial justice in a town where there were no people of color was unpopular. My father, who left the army largely a pacifist, hated war and the military. He told me that if the Vietnam War was still being waged when I was eighteen and

I was drafted, he would go to prison with me. To this day I have images of sitting in a prison cell with my dad.

My father was, finally, a vocal and early supporter of the gay rights movement. His youngest brother was gay. He understood the pain of being a gay man in America in the 1950s and 1960s. The rest of my father's family disowned my uncle. We were the only family my uncle and his partner had. My father's outspokenness about gay rights defied the official policy of the Presbyterian Church.

By the time I was in college at Colgate University, my father had a church in Syracuse. When he found that Colgate, which was an hour from Syracuse, had no gay and lesbian organization he brought gay speakers to the campus. My father encouraged the gay and lesbian students to form a formal campus organization. They were too intimidated – not surprising given Colgate's outsized football program and fraternity system—to do so. This was a problem my dad solved by one day taking me to lunch and telling me, although I was not gay, that I had to found the school's gay and lesbian group—which I did. I used to go into the dining hall and the checker would take my card and had it back to me with saying "faggot."

I saw my father, who I admired immensely, attacked for taking what were moral stances—stances that defied the institutional church where he worked and the values of the community in which we lived. I understood at a young age that you are not rewarded for virtue. Virtue must be its own reward. I saw that when you do what is right it is not easy or pleasant. You make enemies. Indeed, if you take a moral stance and there is no cost, it is probably not that moral. This was a vital lessen to learn as a boy. It prepared me for how the world works. I saw that when you stood with the oppressed you were usually treated like the oppressed. And this saved me from disillusionment. I saw my father suffer—he was a very gentle and sensitive man—when he was attacked. And here personality comes into play. I was born with an innate dislike for authority—my mother says that part of the reason she agreed to send me to boarding school was because I was "running the house"—and thrived on conflict. My father did not. He paid a higher emotional price for defiance.

### Where were you sent to school?

I was given a scholarship to attend a boarding school, or pre-prep school, in Deerfield, Massachusetts called Eagle-brook when I was 10. I went to Loomis-Chaffee, an exclusive boarding school—the Rockefellers went there—after Eagle-brook. The year I graduated from Loomis-Chaffee, John D. Rockefeller III was our commencement speaker.

Boarding school made me acutely aware of class. There were about 180 boys at Eaglebrook, but only about ten percent were on scholarship. Eaglebrook was a school for the sons of the uber-rich. I was keenly aware of my "lower" status as a scholarship student. I saw how obscene wealth and privilege fostered a repugnant elitism, a lack of empathy for others and a sense of entitlement.

C. Wright Mills understood how elites replicate themselves. The children of the elites are, as Mills pointed out in *The Power Elite*, shaped not so much by the curriculum of exclusive schools but by intimate relationships with teachers, who often went to the same schools and prep schools, and by each other. This acculturation takes place through sports teams, school songs and rituals, shared experiences, brands and religious observances, usually Episcopalian. These experiences are often the same experiences of the boys' fathers and grandfathers. It molds the rich into a vast extended fraternity that, because of these unique experiences, are able to communicate to each other in a subtle code. No one outside this caste knows how to speak in this code. This is what Gatsby finds out. He can never belong.

### Who were some of the names you went to school with?

The Mellons, the Buckleys, the Scrantons, the Bissell family, the son of the former Supreme Court Justice Thurgood Marshall and others. A friend of mine's father owned Cartier's jewelers, along with K-Mart and other businesses. I was at the estate of Governor Bill Scranton, who was the Republican governor of Pennsylvania and later a UN ambassador, and watched him come home from work in a helicopter. I had never seen an indoor swimming pool that big.

The rich have disdain for anyone who does not belong to their inner circle. They believe that their wealth and privilege is conferred upon them because of their superior attributes. They define themselves not by what they are in private—in private they are usually bastards—but by the public persona created for them by publicity. They see their possessions and power, which in most cases they inherited, as natural and proper because they believe they are inherently better than others. Balzac said that behind every great fortune lies a great crime. He got that right.

All these families—the Mellons, the Rockefellers, the Carnegies, the Morgans—started out as gangsters. They hired gun thugs to murder union organizers and strikers. We had the bloodiest labor wars in the industrialized world. Hundreds of workers were killed. Tens of thousands were blacklisted. These oligarchic families pillaged, looted and ruthlessly shut down competitors. Their grandsons were sitting next to me in class at Eaglebrook in their school blazers, which by the way could only be purchased at Lord and Taylor.

The refinement of the rich is a veneer. They can afford good manners because they use others—including the machinery of state—to carry out their dirty work. They often know the names of the great authors and artists, but they are culturally and intellectually bankrupt. They are consumed by gossip, a pathological yearning for status and obsessed by brands and possessions—mansions, yachts, cars, gourmet food, clothes, jewelry or vacations at exclusive resorts. They epitomize the cult of the self and the unchecked hedonism that defines a consumer society. They talk mostly about money—the money they made, the money they are making and the money they will make. They are philistines.

My mother's family was from Maine. I spent most of my summers with her family, fishing and hunting. They were working class. My grandfather worked in a post office. One of my uncles—who had fought in the South Pacific in World War II—came back destroyed physically and psychologically. We did not have an understanding of Post Traumatic Stress Disorder. He suffered alone. He was an alcoholic and lived in a trailer. He worked in my great-uncle's lumber mill. But this was only because he was family. Once he was paid, he often disappeared to drink away his paycheck. He reappeared when his money ran out. Another uncle, who was the soul of decency, was a plumber. Many of my relatives, especially my grandfather, were quite intelligent. But none of them had much of an education. My grandfather had to drop out of high school to work his sister's farm after her husband died.

Going back and forth between that world of an elite prep school and this mill town in Maine—Mechanic Falls—I realized that in terms of native intelligence and aptitude, there were people in my family who were as gifted as anyone in my prep school. The difference was that they, like most of the working poor, were never given a chance. And that is what it means to be poor in America. You don't get a chance while the rich get chance after chance after chance.

Look at George W. Bush, a man of limited intelligence and dubious morals. He was a drunk, a cocaine addict, went AWOL from his National Guard unit, and never really held much of a job until he was 40. And he ends up as president. Affirmative action is alive and well, at least for the rich. They know how to take care of their own. And it does not matter how mediocre they are.

**You obviously were closely observing your fellow students' in their native habitats. When you speak of their "disdain" you mean the attitude that these rich kids had toward their servants?**

Yes, I watched how the elites and the children of the elites treated those "beneath" them. I saw my classmates—boys of eleven or twelve—order around adults who were their servants, cooks and chauffeurs. It was appalling. The rich lack empathy for those who are not also rich. Their selfishness makes friendship, even among themselves, almost impossible. Friendship for them is defined as "what's in it for me." They are conditioned from a young age to kneel before the cult of the self. I do not trust the rich. To them everyone is part of their elite club or, essentially, the help. It does not matter how liberal or progressive they claim to be. I would go back to Maine and it would break my heart. I knew what my classmates thought of people like my relatives. I also knew where I came from. I knew whose side I was on. And I have never forgotten. My family was a great gift. They kept me grounded.

**Did your rich friends ever visit you where you lived?**

No.

### Is that because you didn't want them to?

(*Pauses*) Probably. I've never thought about it. I didn't see my family very much. My father worked on the weekends. I used to go to New York with a friend of mine —this is the boy whose father owned Cartier's. His father would send the Rolls Royce down on Friday with the chauffeur so we could go to New York for the weekend. There wasn't really the opportunity for me to have friends over. I lived several hours from the school. But I felt it. When my father picked me up in his old Dodge Dart, classmates would be getting into their limousines.

### Were you embarrassed?

I don't know that I was embarrassed, but I was conscious of it. I didn't like these people. I didn't want to have a limousine, but you were once again called out as the scholarship kid. The world of the rich is very hierarchical. It is built on gradations of wealth. Some scholarship kids, maybe most, desperately wanted to join the elites—that's the story of Gatsby. They were terrible conformists, aping the manners and attitudes of rich classmates. I loathed the rich.

### Why do you think your parents—who were from modest backgrounds and were involved in social activism—sent you to privileged schools like this?

There were a few reasons. My father was at war with the local public school authorities. We had in our community a group of very poor, mixed-race people—probably a mix of white, Indian and black, known in racist slang as *sloughters*. They lived in remote areas outside the village. When the kids from these families got into trouble—and this gets back to my point about how the poor at best get once chance – the principal expelled them. The only person these families could turn to was my father, the local minister. My father hated the principal, who was destroying the lives of these children by denying them an education. So my father was finally banned from entering the school— I think they put a restraining order on him. He was not violent, but he could get angry, especially when children were being hurt.

My mother was teaching in a neighboring village. My parents transferred my sister to her school. I was sent to boarding school, something I never considered for my own children. It was out of Dickens. The youngest boys were bullied by older boys. I fought back, which meant they usually left me alone. I was, however, in a few fights. I still have chipped teeth and once ended up in the hospital with internal bleeding. Boys that did not fight back were crushed. My closest friend at Eaglebrook, a sensitive and sweet boy who should have never been sent to boarding school, committed suicide as a teenager. He may have been gay. The bullying was an accepted part of the culture. Boys were supposed to be tough, not to whine or complain. They were expected to stand up for themselves, to become "men."

I knew about a half dozen boys who were molested by teachers. These schools, where boys and teachers interacted in the classroom, on the athletic fields, in the dining halls and in the dormitories were a paradise for pedophiles. The response of the school was always the same—cover it up. When I was about twelve, my room was next to the apartment of the teacher—we called them masters—on our dorm floor. After lights out at 9:30, he would usher a boy down the hall into his apartment. When we came back from Christmas that year, he and the boy had disappeared. No one said a word. These boarding schools are as culpable in hiding and perpetuating sexual abuse as the Catholic Church.

My father had grown up with old money, although by the time he was an adult the money was gone. He came from an established family—his ancestors settled East Hampton, New York in 1650—so he knew the world of prep schools. He always wore Brooks Brothers suits, although they were an extravagant expense for a Presbyterian minister. He knew the culture of the elites and had contacts among them. I was also gifted academically. Education was important in our family. There was the assumption that these schools would provide a superior education.

### So after prep school, you continue your elite education at Colgate?

Yes, but when I went to Colgate, it was not what it is now. When I went, because I was a resident of New York State, there was generous state scholarship money for students like me. There was a New York State program for lower income students called Tuition Assistance Program. There were regent scholarships. I pretty much went to Colgate for free. About 60 percent of the kids at Colgate were on scholarship. Since then, it has become an elite outpost of places such as Greenwich, Connecticut—but it wasn't like that when I was there. It was a healthier place. I was quite happy there. I had been a very good long distance runner in high school and expected to run in college. My coach had gone to Colgate. It was the only school I applied to. My career as a runner was cut short by injuries. I ended up doing a lot of theater in college, especially Shakespeare.

### You graduate from Colgate in 1979 and go on to Harvard Divinity School—at that time did you

***think you would follow in your father's footsteps and become a minister?***

Yes, although by nature I was a writer. I dictated stories to my mother and she typed them when I was four and five. I always loved books. I wrote stories and poems until I was a teenager. I started an underground newspaper that was eventually banned. When Loomis-Chaffee launched a campaign to raise a few hundred thousand dollars to renovate the chapel, I went up to the squalid living quarters of the kitchen workers although students were forbidden. I took pictures and wrote a story about the conditions endured by the kitchen staff. I waited until the commencement issue to publish it for maximum embarrassment. It worked. The living quarters were renovated. The kitchen staff chipped in to put up a small plaque in my honor. It was an early lesson about the social good that journalism could accomplish.

At Colgate, I had gotten a job the summer after my junior year as an unpaid intern on the House Subcommittee for International Development. I wrote a case study of the corporation Gulf & Western and how it was breaking the unions that were organizing against their sweatshops in the Dominican Republic. Union organizers were being routinely assassinated. Gulf & Western eventually sent a couple guys in suits to meet with the Congressman Michael Harrington, and I was fired from my unpaid internship. I hastily collected $220 dollars from the other interns and hitchhiked to Miami. I flew to the Dominican Republic. I wrote up the story and it was set to appear in the Outlook section of the *Washington Post*. But Gulf & Western, which owned Paramount Pictures, threatened to pull advertising and the paper killed it. I got it published in *The Christian Science Monitor*.

I loved reporting and writing. But I couldn't reconcile American journalism's supposed objectivity and neutrality with the imperative of social justice. At Colgate, I had been very influenced by my religion professor, Coleman Brown, who had worked in East Harlem as a minister. And there was my father. I decided I would be an inner city minister.

I moved across the street from a housing project in the Roxbury section of Boston and ran a church for two-and-a-half years. I commuted to Cambridge to go to divinity school. But I never stopped writing. Writing, for me, is like breathing.

## What were some of the issues you were dealing with in Roxbury?

Racism. Violence. Poverty. Homelessness. Rape. Prostitution. Domestic and child abuse. Drug and alcohol addition. Police violence. Mass incarceration. Welfare. Probation. Failed schools.

I preached on Sunday and ran a youth group. I missed classes almost every Friday because I was in juvenile court. I didn't understand institutional racism until then, all the ways society keeps the poor *poor*. And I had never experienced this level of human suffering, especially the hell endured by people addicted to substances. Poverty, as George Bernard Shaw wrote, is "the worst of crimes. All the other crimes are virtues beside it." Roxbury put race at the center of my understanding of America.

Roxbury is also where I developed my deep dislike for liberals. I was a Presbyterian seminarian, but the church had abandoned the poor with white flight. My classmates at Harvard Divinity School sat around talking about empowering people they'd never met. They liked the poor, but they didn't like the smell of the poor. They would pick coffee for two weeks in Nicaragua with the Sandinistas and spend the rest of the semester talking about it—but they wouldn't ride

20 minutes on the Green Line to where people were being warehoused like animals. I grew increasingly disenchanted with the liberal church and with liberal institutions like Harvard Divinity School. I decided I'd be an inner city cop. I took the police civil service exam.

### Why a cop?

Because I saw that a good cop could make a difference. We had a few.

**This is Adam Walinsky's line, who became an advisor to urban police departments after working as a young Senate aide to Bobby Kennedy. He spent years trying to get the police to function more as inner city social workers.**

Exactly. About 60 percent of all police calls are for domestic disputes. There was this one cop, he was white and his wife was black. He cared—most of them didn't. So I took the exam, there were 50 openings in the department at the time. Kevin White was the mayor. It later came out in his FBI indictment that he gave 48 of the jobs to the children of his cronies in South Boston. It was nepotism. It was rigged. I didn't get the job, even though I scored 98 percent.

# II. Central America: Journalism as a Mission

***How did you end up in Central America?***

During my second year at Harvard, I had developed a friendship with Robert Cox who had been the editor of the *Buenos Aires Herald*, Argentina's English-language newspaper. During the Dirty War in Argentina the military junta disappeared 30,000 of its own citizens, and Cox printed above the fold in the paper the names of *los desaparecidos*, the disappeared. He himself was finally disappeared. He survived only because he was a British citizen. The British government intervened to get him out. Afterwards, he had to leave the country. He was a Nieman Fellow at Harvard. Bob showed me the power of great journalism. He showed me that there was a place for a conscience. He gave me the collected essays, letters and journalism of George Orwell. These four volumes became my secular bible. Orwell, like James Baldwin, used writing as a weapon against lies, abuse of power and injustice. They also cared about the musicality of language.

I decided I would go to Latin America as a reporter. I would fight fascism. Augusto Pinochet ruled Chile. There was a military dictatorship in Argentina, Efrain Rios Montt was massacring indigenous communities in Guatemala. The death squads in El Salvador were slaughtering between 700 and 1,000 people a month.

I left Harvard to study Spanish at the Maryknoll language school in Cochabamba, Bolivia. I freelanced for the *Washington Post* and other publications. I covered the Falklands War from Buenos Aires for NPR. I was not planning to go back to school, but I had a full scholarship from Harvard. My parents, who both had seminary degrees, were apoplectic. So I returned to finish my Master of Divinity—but as soon as I graduated, I went to El Salvador to cover the war. This was the Reagan era. Most of Central America was a war zone. The United States was arming and supporting the military regimes. The peasants, many of them landless and indigenous, were fighting back.

### Why didn't you go to these war-torn countries as a minister? There were a number of socially active clergy members there.

I was by nature a writer. It was as a writer I was meant to express myself. Baldwin had this dilemma. He said he left the pulpit to preach the Gospel. Although I was not public about it, I have always considered myself deep down inside a preacher. It was how I relate to the world.

Preachers, the good ones, like the good reporters, care about truth. Truth and news are not the same. Reporters manipulate facts. Those that are honest manipulate facts to tell the truth. Those that care more about their careers manipulate facts to placate the powerful and obscure the truth. I may have been rejected for ordination, but I saw this as my calling. So did my father.

I went before my ordination committee when I graduated from Harvard—in the Presbyterian Church you must be approved for ordination before you go to seminary. The committee asked me, "What's your call?" I told them, "I'm going to go to El Salvador and be a freelance reporter and cover the war." There was a long pause. The committee chairman said, "We don't ordain journalists."

My dad, who had been a parish minister for 30 years, was seated outside. I told him what happened. I am sure it was hard for him. I had fulfilled all the academic requirements to be ordained. He said, "Well, you're ordained to write." Stephen Kinzer—he and I covered Central America together—once said to me, "You're not really a reporter, you're just a minister pretending to be a reporter." He figured it out.

### And you didn't take that as a put down?

No, no. I consciously put myself in places where I could amplify the voices of the oppressed. This came out of my calling. I didn't want to cover the State Department. I didn't want to go to Washington. I didn't hang around in war zones with the officers or the generals. The assignments I sought most other reporters did not want. They were difficult and dangerous. And they placed me among the poor and the marginalized.

Later in my career, when I was at the *New York Times* and I told the executive editor, Joe Lelyveld, that I wanted to go to Sarajevo at the height of the Bosnian war, he said, "Well I guess the line begins and ends with you." Forty-five foreign reporters had been killed by then in Bosnia, dozens wounded. I never had much competition for these jobs.

***Who are the other reporters you had respect for while you were in Central America? Ray Bonner?***

Yes, Ray. There were several good reporters. Kinzer was good. Sam Dillon at the *Miami Herald*. The Reagan administration really went after those of us who aggressively reported on the war. They tried to discredit our reporting with our editors and sabotage our careers.

***And the* New York Times *executive editor at the time didn't help.***

Abe Rosenthal. I wasn't with the *Times* in Latin America, I began freelancing and then ended up at the *Dallas Morning News*. But yes, Rosenthal saw the world through the simplistic and binary lens of the Cold War. He turned the *Times* into an echo chamber for the neocons and the elites. The reporters and columnists who perpetuated the fiction about a communist takeover in Central America were given a platform. Those, like Ray, who documented the murderous rampages of these regimes were often pushed out.

There is a class of reporters—they show up in every war—who rarely go into the field. They dutifully report what the US Embassy and the military feed them. They spend the war in hotels. They pretend to be war correspondents. They clamor for more briefings, press conferences and dog-and-pony shows. These courtiers made up the vast bulk of the press during the first Gulf War. They go where the military tells them to go. They report what the military tells them to report. They want press restrictions. The more the better.

Those who amplified the views of the embassy in El Salvador created huge problems for us. We had one woman who was working for the *New York Times*, she almost never went out into the field. And because her narrative was so different from ours, and because it was in the *Times,* we were often challenged by our editors. They kept asking us why there was such disparity between the *Times* reporting and our reporting. The power of the *Times,* at least then, was that it set the news agenda for everyone.

*Why won't you name these journalists who collaborated with the Reagan administration line? Wouldn't it be beneficial for journalism to out these sorts of people?*
Many of them are teaching journalism these days. I'm not joking.

*That's ironic.*
Not really.

*So why won't you name them, so journalism students can avoid taking their classes?* (laughs). *That's what Carl Bernstein did by naming many prominent reporters that were working for the CIA, in his famous* Rolling Stone *article back in the '70s? Some of the principal culprits who covered Central America in a way that reflected the Reagan line are well-known.*
The *New York Times* correspondent who was in El Salvador when I arrived now teaches journalism at Berkeley. She was scared. For that reason I do not want to name her, although her reporting obscured the truth on behalf of the US government. Shirley Christian, who covered Latin America for the *Miami Herald* and then the *Times,* however, was different. She was a friend of Reagan national security advisor Ollie North. She was an extreme ideologue. She was hired away from the

*Miami Herald* by Abe Rosenthal to, in essence, demonize the left in Central America, defend the military regimes, and especially the US-backed Contra rebels in Nicaragua, and discredit our reporting. She's someone I'd name. Of course, she now teaches journalism. I think the other reporters who played along with the administration just didn't want to be killed, but they shouldn't have been there. Only about ten or fifteen percent of reporters in any war zone actually spend much time in the field. War photographers are more honest. They have to get out to get the pictures. And when the shooting starts they often have to stand up. The rest of us are hugging the dirt.

**Meanwhile, Rosenthal was taking good, aggressive reporters like Ray Bonner out of Central America.** Yeah, Ray, who—along with Alma Guillermoprieto of the *Washington Post*—broke the story of the El Mozote massacre where the Salvadoran army slaughtered 900 villagers in December 1981. Ray and Alma really pissed off the Reagan people. And so the *Times* under Rosenthal brought Ray back to New York. They did what they always do at the *Times*— they gave him an awful job to humiliate him. That's how they push you out. [Ed. note: Bonner, several years later, was allowed to write for the *New York Times* on a freelance basis.] They make your life miserable. The other reporters and editors, who do not want to be tainted, treat you like a leper. That's how they pushed out Sidney Schanberg who ran the city desk after he came back from covering the conquest of Phnom Penh by the Khmer Rouge. Schanberg ran stories about the homeless, the poor, mentally ill sleeping on heating grates and the developers who were forcing families out of their rent-controlled apartments.

**Even though he'd won a Pulitzer Prize for the newspaper, for his reporting on the war in Cambodia.**
He angered the developers—the publisher's friends. Rosenthal began calling Schanberg the paper's resident "Commie" and addressed him as "St. Francis." Rosenthal, who met William F. Buckley almost weekly for lunch along with the paper's publisher, Arthur Sulzberger, got rid of him.

**So not even the Pulitzer could protect him?**
They don't care. If anyone knows how fixed the Pulitzers are, it's the editors at the *Times*. I was part of a *New York Times* team that won the Pulitzer for our coverage of global terrorism. I watched the *Times* rig them year after year. The *Times* gives a lot of money to the Columbia Journalism School, which oversees the Pulitzers. The committee in return showers the paper with Pulitzers. It may be better now. I don't know. But when I was at the paper it was disgraceful. One year the *Times* war correspondent John Burns wasn't on the short list. The editors had a fit. He not only magically appeared on a new short list but won. Most people don't get awards because they're great reporters, look at Thomas Friedman. They get awards because the establishment wants to validate them. I know who makes up these committees. Robert Scheer [former *Ramparts* magazine writer and editor, *Los Angeles Times* reporter, and founder of *Truthdig*] never got a Pulitzer. He could eat most reporters at the *Times* for lunch.

**So let's return to your journalism career. You distinguished yourself enough in Central America for the big newspapers to begin to take note.**
The *Times* didn't take note at that point, but the *Washington Post* offered me a job when I was covering the war.

I traveled a lot in El Salvador with the army and the FMLN rebels. I broke some major stories.

So the *Post* offered me a job, but they said I'd have to come back to work on the metro desk and cover Maryland. I had no interest in being a metro reporter. I wanted to cover the war.

### What were some of your bigger stories in Central America?

When the International Committee of the Red Cross would go into conflict zones in El Salvador and hand out food and medical care, they'd have to inform the Salvadoran army a week in advance. I found out the army was using this information to set up roadblocks. They would tell the Red Cross workers there was fighting and they couldn't go down the road. Meanwhile, they were surrounding the peasants, whom they considered disloyal masses who were supporting the rebels, and killing them. I also broke stories about corruption in the Salvadoran army, about colonels taking USAID food and selling it. I got access to a captured trove of FMLN documents. Plus, all the daily stories I was filing on the death squad killings and massacres that I usually had to get to on foot.

### Were you ever threatened by the death squads?

Yes, I had to leave El Salvador three times. The [US] embassy did not want too many dead American reporters. They would inform us they had information that the death squads were going to kill us. I'd fly off to Costa Rica and stay at a resort called the Mariposa run by two aging New York queens. I'd read. I'd look out at the Pacific for a couple of weeks. Then I'd come back to El Salvador.

I was 24 or 25. I was crazed. I spent five years covering the war. I had a nervous twitch in my face. I had dark circles

CHRIS HEDGES

under my eyes. I had PTSD. I was a mess. When I lived in
Roxbury I was a member of the Greater Boston YMCA box-
ing team. There was one time I leapt over the counter at the
airport in Costa Rica and let loose on a check-in clerk while
they were crating up my dog. I wrote about it in my book,
*War Is a Force that Gives Us Meaning.*\*

I had wanted to stay in Latin America, where I was working for the *Dallas Morning News*. But the paper didn't want
to open a bureau in South America—so they offered me
London or Jerusalem. I didn't want to go to the Middle East
unless I could speak the language. They paid for me to study
Arabic in Switzerland. I later took the Hebrew University
conversational Arabic course and studied Arabic at The British Cultural Center in Cairo.

*Those were the days when even a regional newspa-
per would actually pay to send you to study Arabic.*
Yeah. In the end, my Arabic wasn't great, but it was okay. After
I got to Jerusalem, I broke a couple of big stories. There was
a Jewish Defense League terrorist named Robert Manning
on the run from the FBI—he was living out near Hebron in
the Jewish settlement of Kiryat Arba. He was the suspect in
the 1985 bombing death in California of Alex Odeh, head
of the Arab-American Anti-Discrimination Committee's
western office, as well as other murders. The Israelis insisted

---

\*Hedges wrote: "When I finally did leave [the Central American war
zone], my last act was, in a frenzy of rage and anguish, to leap over the
KLM counter in the airport in Costa Rica because of a perceived slight by
a hapless airline clerk. I beat him to the floor as his bewildered colleagues
locked themselves in the room behind the counter. Blood streamed
down his face and mine…and I carry a scar on my face where he thrust
his pen into my cheek. War's sickness had become mine."

they did not know where he was. I was doing a story on the Committee for Protection and Safety of the Highways in the occupied West Bank. This group was made up of Jewish settlers that would stop Palestinian cars at improvised roadblocks, pull out the passengers, beat them and sometimes shoot them. I was interviewing Manning. He was a large man. He had a huge knife strapped to his leg and was carrying a pistol and an M-16 assault rifle. When I asked him his name he gave me the name of the FBI agent assigned to his case. This was a stupid mistake. I outed him. Israel was forced to deport him. He is serving a life sentence. It was a good story, but those stories can end your life (*laughs*).

I was breaking stories like this—and also not a lot of reporters speak any Arabic. So the *Washington Post* again asked me if I was interested in a job. I called the *Times*, where Stephen Kinzer had been my great champion—he kept telling them to hire me. I told them, "Look, the *Post* is flying me to Washington." They said, "Okay, we'll fly you up to New York after you're in Washington."

### What year is this?

1990. I saw the *Post*. They offered me a job. I went to the *Times*. They offered me a job, although for a little less money. The *Dallas Morning News* suddenly catapulted my salary up to $70,000 a year, which was a lot of money at the time. I took the job at the *Times* because I was clearly a foreign hire—the *Post* wanted to put me on the metro beat. Seven months later the Gulf War started. The paper sent me to Saudi Arabia.

# III. Life at the New York Times

---

**Were you immediately made aware of the power that the Times gave you, as well as its limitations?**
Yes. I didn't abide by the pool system. I defied the rules. I went out alone. The other *Times* reporters were doing what *Times* reporters do best—sucking up to the authorities. They wrote a letter to the *Times* foreign editor saying I was destroying the paper's relationship with the military. I knew the game. I was prepared to quit. I was young enough, I could go to another paper.

**Why were the other reporters pissed off at you?**
They were happily writing pool reports in the hotel. They didn't want to go out. I blew their cover. If I could go out and get stories, why didn't they go out? But [legendary *Times* editor and correspondent] R.W. Apple—Johnny Apple—was overseeing the paper's coverage of the war from Saudi Arabia. When he found out about the letter, he called us all together.

He said, "Look we don't work for the military." He was my great protector. He saved my job. They would have sent me back. Johnny made sure I could stay and report.

**Johnny Apple famously broke the Times' gray lady mold—he was flamboyant, full of himself, a well-known gourmand and dinner party host.**

He had a lot of Falstaff in him. But he cared about the craft. He was an eloquent writer. He respected good reporters. He wasn't going to let the institution destroy me. My colleagues at the *Times,* however, were only one of my problems. The more stories I wrote outside the pool system, the more the Bush administration wanted me silenced.

Dick Cheney—who was secretary of defense then, under George Bush I—demanded that about a dozen reporters who were defying the pool system be expelled. We were called "unilaterals," a new name for our trade. I was high on the list. But they couldn't find me. I was sleeping with Bedouins in the desert. The US military had already arrested me and confiscated my press credentials. But I did not use press credentials. I was there to be a reporter. If I couldn't be a reporter, I would leave. I wasn't going to sit in a hotel and write up press conferences and pool reports. At that point you might as well take a job with the Pentagon.

I entered Kuwait City before it was officially liberated. I drove my jeep while wearing a Marine Corps combat uniform down the six-lane highway leading out of Kuwait City as thousands of Iraqi soldiers in hundreds of vehicles were fleeing north to Iraq. This soon became the highway of death with miles of burned and wrecked vehicles and charred corpses. I was eventually taken prisoner by the Iraqi Republican Guard during the uprising in Basra after the war. I guess you could say I was embedded with the Iraqis.

### And through all this, you managed to file some strong stories.

It was interesting—when I came back home after the Gulf War, even Abe Rosenthal, who was retired by then, told Joe Lelyveld, who replaced him as the *Times* executive editor, that he wanted to meet me. He came down to the newsroom to shake my hand and told me, "You're a great reporter."

### So even Abe Rosenthal respected you as a war reporter. What did that feel like?

Rosenthal had the instincts of a good reporter. The problem was that, like many who rise within institutions, he cared more about his career than his integrity. He oversaw the publishing of the Pentagon Papers. We have to give him that. The publisher, Arthur "Punch" Sulzberger, who—to highlight how the close-knit fraternity of the elites function—went to my Connecticut prep school, was very reluctant. The idols of power, in the end, always atrophy your soul. Editors and the reporters, at least the ones determined to advance within the institution under Rosenthal's eleven-year tenure as the paper's executive editor, slavishly catered to his neocon ideology and numerous prejudices, including his blind support of Israel and virulent homophobia, which is why the paper ignored the AIDS epidemic. By the time Rosenthal retired and started writing a column, he was hysterical.

I'll tell you what did mean something to me. When Homer Bigart [the *Times*' widely respected correspondent who covered World War II as well as the wars in Korea and Vietnam] died around that time, Sidney Schanberg delivered one of the eulogies. He said we don't have to worry, there are still reporters like Homer out there, and named me. Now *that* meant a lot to me. I didn't care about meeting Abe Rosenthal. Bigart was a hero. He was a reporter's reporter. He cared about the truth. He took tremendous risks to report it. He also loathed the paper's hierarchy. He was once at his desk in the *Times* newsroom taking notes for a story about a riot that were being dictated to him by a reporter, John Kifner, from a pay phone. The riot was getting hot. Kifner finally told Bigart, 'Jeez, Homer, I'm going to have to cut off because there's like a hundred people that are going to push this phone booth over on me." "At least you're dealing with sane people," Bigart answered.

**So by the end of the Gulf War, you're in pretty good standing in the Times newsroom.**

Well, yes and no. Because remember, there were a lot of reporters who didn't like me now. The *New York Times* is primarily populated by careerists. They do journalism on the side. The careerists always get you in the end.

**These are the people who belong to the Council on Foreign Relations and will end up at the State Department or the Kennedy School at Harvard or on Wall Street?**

Exactly. They are courtiers. They serve the elites. The elites reward them for their service with television appearances, lucrative book contracts, foundation grants, awards, journalism professorships and highly paid lecture fees. Many "prestigious" careers in journalism are built this way. These reporters spend their working lives as stenographers for the powerful. They are also your mortal enemy. They know you know them for what they are. Your reporting exposes them as mouthpieces for the elites. I had a few friends at the *Times*. I made the paper look good, so the hierarchy liked it, but I certainly had a lot of reporters who didn't like me.

*Still, you keep getting assignments overseas?*
I was sent to Cairo as the Middle East bureau chief.

*How old are you by then?*
Early thirties…pretty young.

*So if you wanted to play the* New York Times *game, you could've kept rising within that hierarchy?*
Reporters like me do not advance at institutions like the *Times*.

*Because?*
As a war correspondent, I was paid to defy authority and often authority that was trying to kill me. War correspondents almost never reintegrate into newsrooms. We don't bow easily before authority. At places like the *Times* you do not advance if you do not pay homage to the powerful and engage in the subtle games for patronage and influence. You have to be willing to incorporate the ideological parameters of the paper into your reporting.

I spent my time in Central America with a backpack sleeping in mud and wattle huts. When I went to Israel, I was mostly in Gaza. I didn't run off to see the Israeli foreign minister. When I covered the Gulf War, I rarely interviewed someone above the rank of lance corporal and slept in the desert. When I was in Bosnia, I traveled in my jeep from village to village or was in Sarajevo under the shelling and sniper fire. Interviewing those in authority was something I had to do as a *Times* correspondent, but I did it as little as possible. I never saw amplifying the lies of the powerful as an important or interesting part of my journalism.

*So you didn't play the game that most Middle East correspondents play. And playing the game was supporting the Israeli perspective if you were with the* New York Times?

Yeah, [*New York Times* columnist] Thomas Friedman is the classic example of how to play the game. I think most of the other reporters there thought I was a bit insane. Clyde Haberman, the *Times* Jerusalem bureau chief, once said, "Hedges will parachute anywhere, with or without a parachute." That was how they saw me. They were not wrong. I had too much of that hyper-masculine bravado that comes with being a war correspondent. I was also acerbic and blunt. This was not part of the paper's culture.

I was covering the war in Yugoslavia. Roger Cohen [another marquee-name, roving correspondent for the *Times*] dropped into Sarajevo as soon as the ceasefire started. He was based in Paris at the time. He had been my predecessor in the Balkans. He asked me what stories I'm working on, and I say, "I'm doing this and this and this and so on." So then I go off into Bosnia somewhere, and while I'm gone, he stole my stories. He was gunning for a Pulitzer for his Balkans reporting.

*He took what you had written?*

No, I hadn't written them yet. He took my story ideas and did them. We later had a dinner in Paris with all the *Times* foreign correspondents. Roger—who's a snake—says to me in front of all the other foreign correspondents and the foreign editor, in this kind of saccharine voice, "Chris, I heard you've been saying things about me behind my back?" And I said "No, Roger, there's nothing I've ever said behind your back I wouldn't say to your face. You're a shit." You don't do that at the *Times*. It shows a failure to exhibit the right decorum.

At the *Times* you knifed your rivals or colleagues in the back, but you do it with finesse and cloying hypocrisy and...

## A certain corporate gentility?

Yes. That's it. The *Times* is a fear-ridden place. But it wasn't fear-ridden for me. I didn't care. I knew reporters who showed up for work and the first thing they did was go to the bathroom and throw up. It was an unhealthy place. These reporters and editors cared so much about having the "imprimatur" of the *New York Times* that the paper was able to carry out sustained forms of psychological abuse.

So on the one hand I protected myself because I didn't play the game. On the other hand it meant I was never going anywhere—in terms of rising within the hierarchy. Never. Those who rose in the paper had to prove over many years that they were pliant and obsequious to power. They had to endure this corporate hazing. They had to prove that the institution came before all else—including their own colleagues. They had to internalize the unwritten motto of the *Times*: *Do not significantly alienate those on whom we depend for money and access.* You can alienate them some of the time. But if you start to alienate them a lot of the time your career is over. This unwritten mantra set vague, undefined boundaries that contributed to the deep anxiety that dominated the newsroom. Reporters had to intuit how far to go and intuit when to back off.

Those that persisted in reporting stories that made the elites uncomfortable, like Charlie LeDuff, who cared about the marginalized and the poor, who wanted to write about issues such as race and class, increasingly had to run into walls erected by the editors. You either conform or, as Charlie did, quit. The *Times* consciously caters to an audience of roughly 30 million people it has defined as the country's economic and political elite. It does not care about the middle class. It does not care about the working class. And it certainly does not care about the poor. The bulk of the paper, with its special sections such as Styles or Home, addresses the concerns of the rich—maintaining a second house in the Hamptons. Those sections expose its bias.

Reporters who are too obtuse, or too stubborn, to conform become management headaches. If they persist, they are pushed out. This is why, I expect, most people at the *Times* are so unhappy. They have surrendered their independence and often their integrity. They are nervous about crossing the line that will see them singled out. It is a very hard high-wire walk they have to negotiate.

**So the fear that gripped these men and women in the newsroom came from the fact they couldn't see a life for themselves beyond the New York Times. It was the end-all and be-all?**

Yes, it was just like Harvard. The attitude was not we are lucky to have you. It was you are lucky to be here. And since so many people at the *Times* had worked so hard to get there, they bought into this attitude.

**And for you, you could imagine a life outside the Times.**

Yes, I cared far more about what I covered. I wanted to make voices that were shut out heard. This pretty much guaranteed that I would have to eventually find a life outside the *Times*.

**But there must have been occasions when you appreciated working for a newspaper with the power of the Times.**

Of course—I used the power of the *Times*, but I didn't allow the institution to own me. And that's the tragedy of the paper.

You have a lot of talent at the paper. But they are utterly deferential to authority. They invest tremendous energy into finding out what editors like them or whether their stock at the paper is going up or down. It's a Byzantine court. I was the last person to hear the institutional gossip. It saved me from anxiety. But it also hurt my career. I didn't know what was going on. I would get blindsided and not know it was coming.

### When did the power of the Times help you as a reporter?

All the time. It opens a lot of doors. People return your calls. The institution is powerful enough to provide protection and the resources for protection. I had a $100,000 armored car in Bosnia and Kosovo, thousands of dollars of body armor, satellite phones, translators, drivers. Money was not an object. I walked around with thousands of dollars—in the former Yugoslavia the currency was German Deutschemarks— wrapped up in rubber bands in my pocket.

When I was taken prisoner by the Iraqi Republican Guard in Basra, I disappeared. Although the Iraqis were holding me, they denied knowing what had happened to me. This, by the way, is very dangerous. It means that if you are too much baggage, you can be disposed of quickly and no one is responsible. The *Times* got General [Norman] Schwarzkopf to call the head of the Iraqi army. They got [Soviet leader Mikhail] Gorbachev to call Saddam Hussein. They even got the pope to call the foreign minister, Tariq Aziz, who was a member of the Chaldean Catholic minority in Iraq. Then, after I was released, the publisher had to pay the rental company $ 30,000 dollars for the jeep the Iraqis stole from me. I was in violation of the rental agreement.

*You talked earlier about how you didn't follow the pattern of Middle East bureau chiefs at the* Times *in how you covered Israel—can you explain that a bit more?*
When I visited Israel [from the *Times'* Cairo office], I lived in Gaza. In those days Gaza did not have a hotel. I lived in a run-down boarding house. Most reporters, especially *Times* reporters, didn't want to go to Gaza. It was physically uncomfortable—I don't know if it was that dangerous, but it wasn't pleasant. The *Times* ran my stories almost always on the front page. They did not bury them. Most reporters drove down from Jerusalem, went through the Israeli checkpoint, stayed for a few hours to get the dateline and were home for dinner. They wrote canned stories, stories that had already been written in your head on the drive down from Jerusalem. This meant that the real stories rarely got out.

If the Israelis bombed Gaza I'd go into the streets and count the bodies. The Israelis were furious. But what could they do? I was there. It blew a hole in the fiction they put out about surgical strikes.

*So Israel's official reports would minimize the casualties?*
They lied. Constantly. They claimed not to target civilians while using their air force, tanks, naval gunships and heavy artillery to obliterate civilian neighborhoods. Their dishonesty is quite breathtaking.

*When it comes to moments in your newspaper career like this, did you see yourself as more than a journalist—as someone, perhaps from your religious background, who was bearing witness?*
Yes. I was clearly bearing witness. This is why I took the risks I took. But I also, like all good anarchists, distrusted all

forms of power, even those that were ostensibly on the left or claimed to represent the oppressed.

I covered the war in Kosovo. I spent my time reporting on the suffering meted out to Kosovar Albanians by the Serbs. The moment the Serbs pulled out of Kosovo I was reporting on the harassment and murder of the ethnic Serbian minority that remained behind. I never confused institutions or structures of power with the oppressed. I would never lie for a cause.

Journalistic objectivity is a fiction. I can take the same set of facts and spin a story to tell the truth or obscure the truth. Now if you're a careerist, you're going to spin the story in such a way that the power elites, both within the news institution and outside of it, are pleased. That is what they call balance. If you care about the truth, you are going to use those facts to convey the truth. That is what they call advocacy. And for them that is not a compliment.

***Nonetheless, you're saying that when it came to your coverage of the Israeli-Palestinian conflict, you were respected enough by your editors that the* Times *ran your stories on the front page—even though your stories ran counter to the Israeli, and perhaps the Washington, line?***

That's what often happens with a foreign bureau—you're almost always in conflict with the powers back home, whether it's the White House, the State Department, the Pentagon, the CIA or the Washington bureau of your newspaper. This became especially true when I covered Yugoslavia and [diplomat] Dick Holbrooke [who was in charge of President Clinton's Balkans policy] tried to discredit everything I wrote. This made things difficult for me back home, because the Washington bureau is always going to give precedence to the official line. Editors and reporters based inside the Beltway are always doing lunch with the power elites. They depend on those lunches for their stories. And my reports from Bosnia–which after the war made clear the war criminals and warlords were still in charge –were irritating Holbrooke, who had invested his reputation in the Dayton peace agreement that ended the war. Holbrooke was the quintessential mandarin. He cultivated social ties with the powerful and the press, especially the hierarchy of the *Times*. He put a lot of energy into discrediting my reporting. I am sure he did damage.

So foreign correspondents like me can file their reports out of Gaza or wherever, but the preponderance of your newspaper's foreign coverage is spewing out of official Washington. The paper gives a lot of play to what the Israelis want to be reported. The Israelis were always giving "intelligence briefings" to Judy Miller [the *Times* reporter who later became infamous for her false reporting on the Iraqi weapons of mass destruction program]. These Israeli briefings saturated the paper.

The point is that, yes, the *Times* prominently played my reports from Gaza, but the weight of the [Israel-slanted] coverage was such that it kind of overwhelmed the reporting from the field.

### Were you somewhat protected from Israeli pressure because you weren't permanently based there?

Yes, I was based in Cairo. I was only in and out of Gaza. During my four years in Cairo, I spent maybe six or seven weeks a year in Gaza. If I had been in Gaza all the time, the Israelis would have pressured the paper to take me out. I was covering the whole region, including Iraq, Jordan, Turkey, Syria, the Gulf states and all of North Africa. So the Israeli government only had to put up with me a few weeks a year.

But yeah, the Israelis and the Israeli lobby in the United States are powerful, deceitful and ruthless.

### Who's an example of a reporter who became an Israeli target?

Ayman Mohyeldin was pulled out of Gaza by NBC under heavy Israeli pressure. He had witnessed the Israeli military's killing of four Palestinian boys on a beach in Gaza. There are many examples. The Israeli government is hypersensitive about anyone, including Israeli reporters, who challenge the official narrative. The Israeli reporters Gideon Levy and Amara Hass are routinely harassed by the Israeli government, have received death threats and are publicly vilified as accomplices of terrorists for writing the truth about the occupation.

### By the time 9/11 occurs, you are finally back in the States. You were burning out by then as a war correspondent?

Yes. I had spent almost 20 years covering war. I was broken. I was a wreck.

### Were you married at that point?

Yes, but you're never home. My wife and two older children were overseas with me. We lived in Zagreb, or in Cairo— but I was rarely home. And when I did come home I was exhausted and often sick.

### This is your first wife, Josyane, with whom you had a son and daughter?

Yeah.

### But you rarely saw your family?

Yeah.

### How old were you by the time you came back to the US?

Let's see…early 40s.

### So you knew you had to change your life.

I told the paper I had to stop. I wanted to take a Nieman fellowship at Harvard and the *Times* didn't want to let me take it. The paper kept you on salary while you were at Harvard. Bill Kovach, who was the head of the Nieman program and had been the head of the Washington bureau at the *Times*, went to New York and met with Lelyveld and said, "Look, this guy has covered war after war for you, you've got to give this to him." And Lelyveld hit the roof. I was on a satellite phone from Kosovo with my editor Andy Rosenthal, Abe's son, who told me that Lelyveld had said, "All right, tell him he can take the Neiman and go to hell." And Rosenthal told me, "I grew up at this paper—don't do it because they are going to fuck you when you come back." And I took it anyway, and went off to Harvard.

Towards the end of my fellowship, I got a call from Lelyveld. He asked me what I was studying? And I said, "The classics." And he said, "Like Latin?" and I said, "Exactly." There was a long silence and he said, "Well, I guess you can cover the Vatican." I came back, and they fucked me, as Rosenthal warned. They wouldn't give me an assignment.

### Lelyveld was that vindictive?

They are all vindictive. They think they are infallible, like the pope. And there are no shortage of sycophants around them willing to feed their self-delusion. Lelyveld is, I will say in his defense, a fine writer, cares about good reporting and is literate. This is very rare at that level. His successors did a good job of removing all the gravitas, much of which he had promoted, from the paper. [Former Times executive editor] Bill Keller's neocon trolls gutted the Book Review and the Week in Review. Lelyveld didn't let the editors destroy my copy. He reached out to protect the handful of good writers at the *Times*—there aren't that many there. He also hired me.

### And, of course, you were known to be difficult.

I was difficult. I was hired to be difficult. I had been difficult in numerous war zones around the globe for two decades. That is how I did my job and got my stories. You can't turn that off in a newsroom. When I returned from Harvard, it was like the old Soviet Union. You're a member of the Politburo and then one day you suddenly get sent to Kazakhstan. So I sat at home and read Dostoevsky. I can remember Lelyveld saw me in the newsroom after I had been called back and said, "You still remember how to write a story?" Stuff like that. I was on the "outs." They wanted to make me do penance. It is like obedience training for a dog.

### Because you were maybe a little abrasive? [smiles]

I was abrasive. Without question.

### What year was this?

2000.

### And then 9/11 happens.

Right. So 9/11 happens.

### And by then Howell Raines has taken over from Lelyveld as executive editor.

Right. And I speak Arabic. So I'm assigned to the hijackers.

*By the way, what was your relationship with Raines like?*

Raines had no business running a newspaper. He and his managing editor, Gerald Boyd, were driven by naked ambition and self-promotion. This is not unique. But they were also insecure and incompetent. They promoted the con artist, Jason Blair, who fabricated and plagiarized stories. They empowered Judy Miller and Michael Gordon to publish the lies of the Bush administration to justify the Iraqi invasion. They pushed aside talented reporters and editors when they were not obsequious enough. It was all about who could grovel and flatter them the most. The newsroom, not made up of natural rebels, rose up in revolt. Raines and Boyd lost control of the paper,.

*But before all that, you're part of the team that covers 9/11?*

Yeah, I reported from cities such as Paterson, New Jersey where six of the hijackers had been living. Then I was sent to Paris to cover Al Qaeda in Europe and the Middle East.

*And you're finding out that the facts on the ground don't go along with the emerging Bush-Cheney story line, that Saddam Hussein was behind 9/11.*

The French government was apoplectic about the Bush administration's decision to invade Iraq. It made no sense to them. They knew Iraq had nothing to do with the attacks, that its army and military was severely degraded. Iraq was not a threat to its neighbors, much less to Europe and the United States. It did not have weapons of mass destruction. The French government, since I was with the *Times*, gave me carte blanche. I could go into the ministry of interior and ask for intelligence files. They were desperate to stop the war. It is a pity they failed.

### They saw this train running out of control, driven by Cheney and his crowd.

Yes, and Al Qaeda was the problem, not Iraq. They had long experience with Islamic radicalism starting in the 1980s with the Paris Metro bombings by Algerian terrorists. I would come back to New York for meetings with the *Times* investigative unit. Judy Miller was part of that group. And the reporters and editors dismissed the French intelligence. They all drank the Kool-Aid. They were sure Lewis "Scooter" Libby—an Eaglebrook graduate, by the way—and the others in Cheney's and Rumsfeld's cabal were telling them the truth. The crazies were not only running the country but the coverage inside the paper.

### You believe that Judy Miller, whose journalism career was eventually ruined, got scapegoated for spreading the WMD propaganda?

Yes, even though Judy Miller epitomizes everything I detest in reporters, but...

### But she wasn't the only one.

That's right, it was an institutional failure at the *Times*. Howell Raines, and his successor Bill Keller and the investigative editors and reporters were all Bush's useful idiots. It was a colossal journalistic failure—equaled by the paper's cluelessness about the 2008 financial crash—that was dumped on Miller. They were all complicit.

***Did any of your reporting that contradicted the Bush-Cheney line about Iraq get into the paper?***

I was covering Al Qaeda. I wasn't covering Iraq. I had one brief foray into that morass.

***Yes, Judy Miller—in her own defense—later said, "Oh, even the great Chris Hedges got snookered by the Iraq story."***

Judy Miller and [investigative journalist] Lowell Bergman were working with Ahmed Chalabi [the Iraqi exile leader who was one of the principal sources behind the false WMD story]. Lowell was a producer at PBS's *Frontline*. There was a joint project between the *Times* and *Frontline*. I was in Paris or somewhere in Europe. Lowell had set up an interview with what he said was an Iraqi defector in Lebanon—but he couldn't go with his camera crew. The *Times* sent me. I didn't vet the guy, I didn't set up the interview. This often happens in big news organizations. You share reporting and information. I did the interview. It later turned out the guy's story [about the Iraqi regime training Islamic terrorists] was bogus.

***So you too played your own small role in the* Times' *disgraceful reporting during the runup to the Iraq War?***

Yes. I have to take responsibility for it. It was my byline.

***Did you ever talk to Bergman about it later?***

No. I didn't have an option to say no.

***You're part of an army.***

Right.

**But you had a history of questioning authority at the Times. Why not on this occasion? Did you get infected a bit by the post 9/11 madness?**

I covered Iraq after the 1991 Gulf war. I reported on the destruction and dismantling by the U.N. inspection teams of Iraq's chemical and biological weapons stockpiles. I knew Iraq's nuclear weapons facilities had been destroyed by US air strikes in the 1991 war. I knew that the Iraqi military machine, starved of funds and spare parts, was falling apart. But I also knew that Saddam Hussein had harbored various terrorists over the years including Abu Nidal. He had ties with Hamas. And he had held a series of meetings with Al Qaeda after his defeat in the 1991 Gulf war.

In 1992, when I was covering the Middle East, the Sudanese leader Hasan al-Turabi set up a meeting between the Iraqi intelligence and Osama bin Laden, who was living in Khartoum. Bin Laden requested the Iraqis provide weapons and training camps in Iraq. Ayman al-Zawahiri, at the time the ideological leader of Al Qaeda, traveled to Iraq that same year for a meeting with Saddam Hussein. He was there again in 1999 to attend the Ninth Islamic People's Congress. He may have made other trips to Iraq. Iraqi intelligence, it appears from documents found after the 2003 invasion of Iraq in the archives of the Iraqi secret service, worked with Zawahiri and Al Qaeda to create the Kurdish Islamic militant group Ansar al-Islam, which was modeled on Hezbollah. Zawahiri, the current head of Al Qaeda, led the Al Qaeda insurgency against American forces inside Iraq after the 2003 invasion.

I did not see the invasion as justified. I believed the Bush administration was lying about weapons of mass destruction. But it was not beyond belief that Saddam was attempting to stoke terrorism against pro-western regimes in the Middle

East and the United States by training and funding Islamic radicals, including Al Qaeda.

The two stories I published out of Beirut about Iraq's supposed training of Islamic terrorists at an Iraqi military training center called Salman Pak, along with the alleged continued imprisonment in Iraq of about 80 Kuwaitis taken hostage during the first Gulf war, were, however, untrue. I went to Beirut with a healthy distrust of Saddam Hussein and, in retrospect, too much trust in the abilities of Lowell Bergman. I had asked US Embassy officials in Ankara if the self-described defector was legitimate and was assured he was. But I should have done a more thorough vetting before I agreed to publish. I did not. This was my failure.

**Of course when Bush finally invades Iraq in April 2003, you are a vocal critic of the war. When do you deliver the infamous speech about the Iraq War at the college commencement ceremony?**
Spring of 2003.

**And you're still on staff at the Times, based in New York?**
Yes.

**And you're invited by this liberal arts college in Illinois, Rockford College, to deliver the graduation speech. Did you have any connection to the school?**
No. I knew that [social reformer] Jane Addams had graduated from there. The new president –who had written his doctoral dissertation on Addams—wanted to get somebody in the activist spirit of Jane Addams. I had breakfast with him at the college and said, "I'm going to be pretty harsh on the war" and he said, "Oh, not a problem."

*This was at a time when people like the Dixie Chicks were being banned from radio and Bill Maher was being fired from ABC for their critical comments about Bush and the war. And you step right into this fire and give a very powerful anti-war speech. And what was the reaction from the crowd that day?*
It was not pleasant.

*How many people were there?*
About a thousand. They hated it. They booed and tried to shout me down...

*And you could hear it loud and clear?*
Yes. At one point they all got up and began singing *God Bless America*. They cut my microphone three times. Two young men from the graduating class got up in their robes tried to push me from the podium. I kept giving the speech. Michael Moore later saw a video of it and said, "I don't know who the actor is in your family, you or your wife." [Ed. Note: Hedges is married to actress Eunice Wong]

*So you kept bulldozing your way through all the sound and fury in the crowd?*
Yeah.

*And did you make it all the way to the end of your speech?*
No, the president said I should, "Wrap it up!" after 18 minutes. Campus security escorted me off the stage before the awarding of diplomas. I was in an academic gown. I told them my coat was in the president's office. They said, "We'll mail you your coat"— which they did. They took me to my

hotel room, waited as I packed my bags and drove me to the bus station. I got on a bus to Chicago.

**So you escaped the tar and feathers. But you certainly felt the madness that was sweeping America in those days.**
Yeah. The amateur video footage of the speech spread like wildfire. My daughter was in elementary school at the time and they were watching some PBS show and suddenly her whole class goes, "Hey look, that's your dad!"

**And what was the fallout at the Times?**
The *Times* felt pressured to respond. The right-wing talk shows and cable shows lynched me hour after hour, day after day. The *Wall Street Journal* ran an editorial denouncing me. The *Times* issued me a written reprimand. Under Newspaper Guild rules this the final step before being fired. Violate the reprimand and you're out.

**What did they say was your violation?**
I had impugned the impartiality of the paper.

**By taking a strong stand against the war—a war which they had helped start, and which they later condemned?**
Right. In contrast, [*Times* reporter] John Burns had taken a stand supporting the war, but he didn't get reprimanded. It wasn't taking a strong stand that was the problem. It was taking a stand contrary to the dominant narrative.

**And so you get this formal reprimand?**
Right.

## And then what happens?

I realize it's terminal. It was not easy. I didn't want to lose my job. But I was faced with a choice. I could muzzle myself in fealty to my career, but to do so would be to betray my father. I could not do that. When I left the building, I knew it was over. I also articulated for the first time what my father had given me—freedom. I did not need the *Times* or any institution to tell me who I was. I knew who I was. I was my father's son.

I negotiated a fellowship with Hamilton Fish at The Nation Institute and left the paper.

## So you quit—you didn't get fired, as some believe.

I did not get fired, as [current *New York Times* executive editor] Dean Baquet reminded me the last time I saw him.

## Do you think you would have been fired ultimately?

I'm not sure. I think many at the paper rolled their eyes and thought, "There he goes again." I didn't sense they wanted to lynch me. They were covering their asses. At the same time, I was often clueless about the internal politics. I could be wrong. Certainly if there was another national incident like Rockford they would have gotten rid of me.

I don't have any animus towards the *Times*. I had a great run. They sent me all over the world. I am much, much happier writing books. I speak and write in my own voice. Financially I have survived. I still read the paper.

# IV. The Seductions of Power

---

*Let's step back and try to put the Times in the broader context of corporate media and the US power structure. As a longtime radical journalist and someone who has operated in opposition to the mainstream media—I'm talking about myself now –working at Mother Jones and founding Salon and so on, I pretty much think the classic leftist analysis of establishment media is the correct one. That is, for all the good, solid journalism done on the ground by individual reporters like you and others, at the top level these institutions are completely and inextricably tied up with other powerful institutions—whether it's Wall Street or the federal government and its national security agencies...*

This is true.

*And so, while institutions like the* Times *often publish great investigative reporting on political and corporate scandals, or criminal labor conditions or environmental abuses, when it comes to fundamental national security issues like are we going to war, they fall in line. Not only fall in line, but usually help promote these military expeditions—and seldom question the assumptions behind major national policy initiatives like the war on terror, whatever that is these days. Or the fundamental assumptions underlying corporatist economic policy.*

All the mainstream media does that.

### Sure, I'm not saying just the Times.

As soon as the war started, the press became abject cheerleaders for the war. They did their "patriotic" duty. This is always what happens, going back to the Crimean War. Phillip Knightley pointed this out in his book, *The First Casualty.* Truth is always the first casualty of war. The early coverage of Vietnam was like this. The coverage only changed when the public perception of the war changed. The established press is always a reactive force despite its claim about being vanguards of truth. Let's be fair, sometimes the Left is cheerleading too, as it did in the Spanish Civil War and in Central America when I was there.

I watched the Left make these mistakes in Nicaragua and El Salvador during the Reagan era. The Sandinistas in Nicaragua and the FMLN rebels in El Salvador were nowhere near as violent or criminal as the military governments in El Salvador or Guatemala or the US-backed contra rebels in Nicaragua. Nonetheless, the Left had a responsibility to be rigorous with the Sandinistas' human rights violations or with abuses by the FMLN. This would have given it credibility when it decried the human rights abuses in El Salvador and Guatemala.

War seduces the Left as much as the Right. Peace activists – they were nicknamed the Sandalistas—came to Nicaragua and went limp in front of the Sandinistas. I lived in Central America. I covered it. I said, "Look, we've got acts of genocide, thousands of death squad killings and massacres in Guatemala and El Salvador. If we refuse to be ruthlessly honest in Nicaragua, where the sins of the regime exist but pale in comparison to what is happening in Guatemala and El Salvador, or if we will not criticize the FMLN, then we become propagandists. We lose our credibility. We make the crimes [of the Reagan-supported contra forces and Central American dictatorships] easier to discredit because we have discredited ourselves. We can't do that." Few listened. They were more concerned about being certified as revolutionaries.

**I assume that's why Orwell is one of your heroes – because, although he was a man of the Left, he unflinchingly confronted the crimes and abuses of the Left in those places where it took power, or where its ideals were corrupted.**

Orwell made this same argument in *Homage to Catalonia*. He included in the book the May 1937 attacks by the Spanish government forces in Barcelona, led by the Spanish Communist Party, which resulted in the bloody suppression of the anarchists in the POUM [*Partido Obrero de Unificación Marxista* or Worker's Party of Marxist Unification]. Orwell fought in POUM militia at the Aragon front and in the street battles in Barcelona. He was eventually wounded, shot through the neck. By June 1937 the POUM offices and newspapers were shut down by the Communists. The POUM leader Andreu Nin was arrested and murdered.

Orwell was incensed that the Left refused to denounce the purge. He was not going to lie on its behalf. Victor Gollancz, who had published Orwell's previous book, *The Road to Wigan Pier*, refused to publish *Homage to Catalonia*. He said it might "harm the fight against Fascism." It was published by another publisher, but had a very limited run and was eventually remaindered. *The Daily Worker* denounced Orwell as "pro-fascist." By the time Orwell died in 1950, the book had sold less than 1,000 copies.

Orwell understood that telling the truth is often a revolutionary act. He had a natural hatred of authority. He knew all authorities lie. He understood that lies were a form of manipulation, a way to turn human beings into objects to be controlled. Lies work in the short term, but in the long term lies destroy your credibility. He would not suppress the truth for a political objective. The truth, and justice, was too precious.

### Talk some more about why Orwell—and Baldwin—inspired you as a reporter and a writer.

Baldwin and Orwell refused to exempt anyone from their withering critique and fierce honesty. This included themselves. Baldwin shone the fierce light of his honesty on black culture, the black church and the black press while Orwell did this to the established Left. They always wrote, as Orwell said, from "a sense of injustice." There was, as Orwell said, always some lie to expose, some fact to which they wanted to draw attention. Their honesty, their religious commitment to the truth, freed them from dogma and ideology. "Good prose," Orwell wrote, "is like a windowpane."

Orwell and Baldwin were also acutely aware of the mystery of human existence. They ripped back the visible reality to, as Baldwin said, seek out things unseen. They took nothing for granted. They sought, as Baldwin said, "the heart of every answer" to expose "the question the answer hides." They knew, as Baldwin wrote, that when we cannot tell ourselves the truth about our past, we become trapped in it. This is especially true about race in America. Our undiscovered self cripples us.

**Orwell's and Baldwin's honesty is in sharp contrast, as you say, to someone like Hemingway, whose war reporting in Spain was blinded by the romance of the Left and other mythologies.**

Hemingway was blinded by his celebrity. He was a terrible reporter. His journalism during the Spanish Civil war was centered on his "manly" experiences in combat. His reports were often hard to believe. They were filled with cliché dialogue and gruesome descriptions of war clearly picked for their shock value. It is widely believed he made a lot of stuff up. During World War II he sent back reports about taking part in fighting as if he was an infantry officer.

He was a flagrant propagandist for the Republicans. He never wrote about the brutal Communist-run prisons, repression, persecutions and wholesale executions of anarchists and socialists, which numbered in the thousands, often by Soviet agents. And we know he knew about them. Soviet agents executed José Robles Pazos, the translator and close friend of John Dos Passos, after being falsely accused of being a "fascist spy," but Hemingway never questioned the official account. It ended his friendship with Dos Passos. Hemingway filed wildly optimistic reports predicting Republican victory long after it was clear the Republicans were headed for defeat. He eventually wrote the truth about the war in his novel *For Whom the Bells Tolls*, but by then the war was over.

The war for Hemingway was a stage in which he was an international star. He was not about to let the truth alienate his relationship with the Republican authorities, or taint the heroic narrative, which fed his celebrity.

Edmund Wilson pointed out that something frightful happened to Hemingway as soon as he wrote in the first person. As an artist he could hold his personality at bay. But in the first person he had no self-restraint. He became, in Wilson's words, "fatuous or maudlin." He was, of course, a huge celebrity. He was always being photographed on a lion hunt, at a bullfight, fishing for marlins off the coast of Cuba or posturing as a war correspondent. His reporting was in service to his image. He was a victim of his own propaganda. He never grew up. He was a perpetual adolescent.

Hunter Thompson suffered from the same personality disorder. You do not want to believe the hype about yourself. It is false, like all manufactured personalities used to create celebrities. It kills you as a writer and an artist. Hemingway's lack of self-criticism and self-awareness ultimately destroyed him. He no longer knew who he was. He ended his life, like Thompson, a parody of himself. They each, of course, committed suicide.

In any case, that's why it's funny that I'm often considered part of the Left because I never pull my punches on the Left. I don't pull my punches for anyone. I stand with people, but not with groups. I stand with people who are oppressed.

**It reminds me of the old Groucho Marx joke. You won't belong to any club that would have you as a member.**

The moment you need adulation you're finished.

**_But always being an outsider, never being embedded with any group or forces can be dangerous._**

True.

### _Give me an example._

I was writing stories out of northern Iraq on internecine fighting between the Kurds. Baghdad put prices on the heads of the handful of reporters in northern Iraq. Since the Iraqis had withdrawn, we were uncovering the crimes of the regime—the huge mass graves, the secret prisons, the torture centers, the videos of executions. I had seven Kurdish bodyguards. We slept in different corners of the room. If somebody burst into the room he couldn't direct the fire at one spot. This was the closest I came to having a weapon. My bodyguards put a 9 mm pistol next to my head when I slept., I was to shoot if someone came through the door firing. I probably would have been killed trying to find my glasses. One night we're listening to a propaganda broadcast, in Kurdish, coming from Baghdad. The announcer read my _New York Times_ story on fighting between the Kurdish factions. My bodyguards became very uncomfortable. It was a difficult moment. But as Orwell knew the only thing we have is our credibility.

# V. Beyond Electoral Politics

*Let's talk about the Obama legacy. Do you share your friend Cornel West's view of him—that he was an Uncle Tom who sold out to Wall Street and the other centers of American power?*

Yes. The facts support Cornel's statement.

*How do you back that up?*

A $7.7 trillion bank bailout and nothing for people who lost their homes—I mean, how is that disputable? Obama did what he was paid to do. He delivered credulous voters into the hands of Wall Street. [Ed. Note: According to a Bloomberg Markets analysis, during Obama's first year in office, the Federal Reserve committed a staggering $7.77 trillion to rescuing the financial system, or "more than half the value of everything produced in the US that year."]

He's worse than Bush. Bush was witless. He was a tool of Cheney and the neocons. But Obama is very intelligent and very cynical. And Obama has not only expanded these wars, especially with drone strikes that include assassinating US citizens, but his assault on civil liberties has been worse than under Bush.

### When did you see that writing on the wall about Obama?

[Former Ohio congressman] Dennis Kucinich gave me Obama's two-year voting record in the Senate. He said, "Read it –it's one corporate giveaway after another."

### Obama's a product of the elite educational system that we were talking about earlier, that you're very familiar with. A bright, middle-class boy who gains entry to the elite world through his education at Punahou School in Hawaii, then Occidental College, Harvard Law and so on.

These elite institutions train you to embrace the shared belief system of the elites. Schools like Harvard exist to perpetuate the plutocracy. Obama was a diligent and obedient pupil.

### So you and Cornel West, who is a friend of yours, saw eye-to-eye about Obama. But you parted company on the 2016 presidential race. He threw himself into the Bernie Sanders campaign, while you backed the Green Party candidate.

Cornel is not blind to Sanders' faults. Cornel believes an insurgency can take back the Democratic Party. I do not. Sanders was never going to be, in his own words, a "spoiler." He always made it clear that he would support the Democratic nominee. This makes him an obstacle to real change. He recites the mantra of the "least worst." He inevitably will become part of the Democratic establishment's campaign to neutralize the Left.

Sanders is, in all but title, a Democrat anyway. He is a member of the Democratic caucus. He votes 98 percent of the time with the Democrats. He routinely backs appropriations for imperial wars and voted for the corporate scam of Obamacare, wholesale surveillance and the bloated defense budgets. He campaigned for Bill Clinton in the 1992 presidential race and again in 1996—and this was after Clinton passed the North American Free Trade Agreement (NAFTA), vastly expanded the system of mass incarceration and destroyed welfare. He campaigned for John Kerry in 2004. He called on Ralph Nader in 2004 to abandon his presidential campaign. The Democrats recognize his value. They reward Sanders for his role as a sheepherder by not running a serious candidate against him in Vermont.

We are never going to carry out deep structural change through the Democratic Party. We have to build movements, including third party political movements, outside these structures.

**Aren't you being too hard on Bernie? He at least brought the rhetoric of the Occupy movement into national electoral politics. Don't you think his messaging about the grotesque wealth gap and the corruption of the political system helped advance the discussion in this country?**

Yes. He did a few of important things. He restored the good name of "socialism" to our political vocabulary. He spoke openly about income inequality and corporate greed. He did not toe the rigid party line on Israel. And he defied the corporate financing of campaigns. These are important steps forward.

*Certainly he was a different political figure than what we've been accustomed to on the presidential stage—an unapologetic democratic socialist who campaigned against the power of Wall Street and Big Pharma and the fossil fuel industry.*

He acknowledged reality. We live in a non-reality-based political system. Trump's success was based on a similar candor. "Sure," he told people, "I gave money to everybody, even the Clintons, because that's how the system works." It's the same with Sanders. He talked about economic inequality and everybody went ecstatic because, a politician is finally acknowledging the obvious! But what was he going to do about it? He wasn't going to nationalize the banks if he became president. And supporting Hillary Clinton is not going to help us wrest back power from corporations.

*He promised to impose much higher taxes on the wealthy and Wall Street speculators.*

Yes, but if we don't get control of the military spending we're finished. We're being hollowed out from the inside like every other empire. We have expanded beyond our capacity to sustain ourselves. Our infrastructure, our public educational system, our social services—everything is crumbling for a reason, we don't have any money for it. It is being consumed by the war machine. And Sanders didn't touch the military-industrial-complex. That would have been political suicide.

*I agree with you on that—by and large, the bloated war state was not part of Bernie's campaign rhetoric.*

There will be no socialism until we dismantle imperialism and dramatically slash military spending power. Martin Luther King understood that.

**So you don't believe that there's any way to turn the energy he generated among young voters and so on into a long-range, progressive movement?**

He raised political consciousness. But he did not create a movement. A movement has to have a bigger goal than electing a candidate. A real movement will only rise outside the Democratic Party, since the Democrats are captive to corporate power. How can you talk about a political revolution and support Clinton? If he had been building a revolutionary movement I would have supported him. His talk of political revolution was as empty as Obama's slogan about hope and change.

**So what do you think his end goal was, then, if he had no intention of creating a movement beyond his candidacy?**

I talked with him about his strategy in fall 2015, when he was getting ready to run.

**You met with him?**

The night before the big climate march in New York. I did an event with Bernie, Bill McKibben, Naomi Klein and Kshama Sawant, the socialist city council member from Seattle. Kshama and I asked him why he wasn't running as a third-party candidate. He said, "I don't want to end up like Ralph Nader." And he's not wrong. The Democrats would have destroyed him if he had challenged the Democratic Party. The corporate media would have ignored him.

So he'll keep his Senate job. He'll keep his seniority in the caucus. But it's cowardly.

**Again, in Bernie's defense, he acknowledged that electing someone like him president would not be**

*enough. Even if you think his rhetoric about this was hollow, he kept saying that we need a revolutionary movement to address the country's fundamental inequities and problems. But you don't seem to put much value in electoral politics, while I see it as a potential way to help build a progressive movement and in some cases to elect people who actually do make a real difference in terms of the public good.*

Voting is meaningless without movements that can pressure those in power and without serious campaign finance reform. We live in what Sheldon Wolin called a system of "inverted totalitarianism." Unlike classic totalitarianism, our system does not find its expression in a demagogue or a charismatic leader but in the faceless anonymity of the corporate state. These corporate forces purport to pay fealty to electoral politics, the iconography and language of American patriotism, the Constitution, but internally have seized all of the levers of power to render the citizen impotent. Even if Sanders had somehow become president, his hands would be completely tied. The centers of power lie outside the system of electoral politics.

*I want to be clear about your position on electoral politics and whether people should be involved at all in the election process. So you reject even left-wing campaigns within the Democratic Party like Sanders'. But you do endorse third-party campaigns, like that of Dr. Jill Stein, the Green Party's 2016 presidential candidate. See, that to me is baffling, speaking of the follies of the Left. Because clearly Stein has not made a dent on public consciousness, not even on the left.*

That's right.

### Her campaign is completely quixotic...

It's because she's a socialist and seeks to build a party that gives a political voice to groups such as Black Lives Matter or the anti-fracking movement. The Green Party platform calls for massive cuts in military spending and a national plan to build a green infrastructure. It backs the BDS [boycotts, divestments and sanctions] movement against Israel.

### But when you're facing a real fascist threat, with the emergence of someone like Donald Trump, as you have acknowledged, is it responsible to throw your support to a fringe candidate who has no hope of stopping this train wreck?

Voting for Clinton and supporting the Democratic Party will not curb the rise of American fascism. Trump did not create the phenomena. He responded to it.

The Democrats, and in particular Hillary and Bill Clinton, are responsible, along with the rest of the Democratic elites, for our being sacrificed on the altar of corporate profit. They engendered this rage. They told the same lies as the Republicans. They fed the same white racism. They exploded our prison population. They destroyed our welfare system—and 70 percent of the original recipients were children. They enabled the corporate coup. They unleashed the predators on Wall Street and in the fossil fuel industry. They colluded to strip us of our civil liberties. They backed endless war and fed the obscene profits of the arms industry and swelled agencies such as Homeland Security. Obama and the Democrats have authorized the assassination of US citizens. They signed into law legislation that permits the military to act as a domestic police force and detain US citizens indefinitely without due process. Obama and the Democratic Party establishment, working with the Republicans, turned us into the most watched, photographed and monitored population in human history. And they are attempting to ram new trade agreements down our throats.

It pays to sell out the citizenry. The Clintons have made more than $153 million for paid speeches alone since 2001. The Democratic Party is awash in corporate cash. And the Obamas will soon, like the Clintons, be multimillionaires.

American politics is anti-politics. Culture wars have replaced political debate. The Democrats co-opted the liberal elites, minorities and unions. The Republican Party embraced the Christian right, nativists and opponents of abortion rights. The Republicans and the Democrats looked at their supporters as useful idiots. It worked for a while. Then, the manipulated and the abandoned rose up. Voters flocked to the Trump and Sanders' political insurgencies.

It was a bankrupt liberal establishment that made possible the rise of totalitarianism in Germany and Russia. From Fyodor Dostoevsky to Hannah Arendt [astute observers have] singled out a failed liberalism as the cause of widespread hopelessness and isolation that led to totalitarianism. They understood that stories of rage begin as stories of despair. Liberalism, by constantly betraying its stated values, destroyed itself. It left the working poor bereft of support. Incremental and piecemeal reform within the system became impossible. When the underclasses turned against the liberal establishment in Weimar Germany or revolutionary Russia, they rejected not only its representatives, but the values liberals claimed to represent. A desperate population searched for a messianic leader who would bring new glory, strength, moral renewal and vengeance.

We can continue to vote for these self-identified liberals, but the problem will only get worse. Trump may disappear. But someone as vile will rise to take his place. The mantra of the "least worse" does not work—look at the steady deterioration in American politics. The "least worst" paves the way for the worst.

***And so yes, the 2016 presidential race devolved into a contest between Hillary Clinton and Donald Trump—which reminds me of what my mother used to say: "Pick your poison." Did the prospect of a Hillary Clinton presidency disturb you any less than a Trump reign?***

The focus on the particular personalities vomited up by the political system distracts the public from the near total transfer of power into the hands of corporations. Trump and Clinton do not have the ability to change our system of inverted totalitarianism, nor do they have the interest. Our political and economic elites—including Trump and Clinton – are hostile to genuine change. They don't work for us. They don't work for the planet. And they are well paid for it.

The wars will still be waged no matter who wins the White House to enrich the arms manufacturers. Wall Street will still carry out its casino capitalism and push us ever closer towards another financial meltdown. The security and surveillance state will still make us the most monitored and watched society in human history. The trade agreements will still be signed to further weaken national sovereignty and send more jobs overseas. The prisons will still swell with the bodies of the poor. Social programs will still be diminished or terminated in the name of authority. These corporate forces lie beyond the control of the state, indeed the state has become the vehicle for the further consolidation of corporate power and profits. We do not have any institutions left that can be authentically called democratic, if we define democratic to mean the expression of the popular will. Civic virtue has been transformed into economic rationality. We have to start rebuilding from scratch outside of the system, including the creation of third parties that openly defy corporate power.

That the Left falls election cycle after election cycle for this charade is a sign of its political immaturity. Plato warned that a failed democracy lays the foundations for a "democratic" despotism. Democracy, at least as myth, does not disappear, Plato says, but becomes the ideological framework by which tyranny is advanced. The presidential face is only the brand on the package of corporate power. Elected officials serve the system. If they do not, they are replaced. If anyone thinks there would be vast differences between Trump and Clinton – each uniquely repugnant—they do not understand how our system works.

# VI. Revolution or Fascism?

**Okay, let's talk about what you think we really have to be doing politically at this point.**

We must do the hard work of stepping outside the system and building our own radical structures to fight back. It will not be easy. We have to build powerful, anti-capitalist movements like Syriza in Greece and Podemos in Spain and *Jóvenes ante la Emergencia* in Mexico. Without powerful grassroots movements we are finished.

I put all my political effort into movements. I was in Denver a few weeks ago to speak to 400 anti-fracking activists. Young activists, clutching their backpacks, were coughing because they had respiratory problems from working in the fracking zones. They had rashes, headaches and nosebleeds. They're not buying the bullshit. I spoke in Washington to about 300 BDS activists. That's where the hope is. Ninety percent of the American electorate did not vote in the primaries. Let's not get too excited about this very expensive and elaborate political theater. If voting was that effective, as Emma Goldman said, it would be illegal.

### Why, after a decade of economic anguish, hasn't America seen the rise of a radical movement, as in these other countries?

This is the focus of my book, *Death of the Liberal Class* The radical Left was destroyed in the name of anti-communism. Howard Zinn in the *People's History of the United States* points out correctly that these radical movements, which never assumed positions of formal power, were the forces that opened up our democratic space. The men who founded this country were mostly slaveholding, white oligarchs. They constructed a system that would make direct democracy impossible—hence the Electoral College and the disenfranchisement of African-Americans, women, Native Americans and men without property as well as the old system whereby senators were appointed by the states. The opening of political space came from radical movements—the abolitionists, the labor movement, the suffragists, and the civil rights movement.

World War I was, as Dwight Macdonald said, the rock on which these movements broke. The state fostered, in Macdonald's words, the ideology of the "psychosis of permanent war." Radical movements were destroyed in the name of the war against Germany and then the war on communism. Populist movements were destroyed by the liberal state, in service to corporate interests.

And so, here in the US, we have been left powerless. In Europe these radical movements, while repressed, were not obliterated. In the United States the destruction was total. We have to start again from scratch. We have to build the kind of new mass movements I saw in countries like East

Germany, where you had half a million people showing up in Alexanderplatz in East Berlin or half a million people showing up in the streets of Prague in Wenceslas Square during the Velvet Revolution, which I also covered.

***Some would say that, even as you build these populist movements, you also have to play the political game or it will play you. They point, for instance, to the crucial appointments a president makes, starting with the Supreme Court.***

They said that about Obama too, and look where we are. These are ornamental issues. We have to talk about, as Wolin writes, the system of inverted totalitarianism and how to destroy it.

***All right, so let's talk about Sheldon Wolin, whom by the way I took a class from, way back when I was a freshman at the University of California in Santa Cruz. With his concept of inverted totalitarianism, Wolin makes a kind of new argument for the banality of evil—he says that tyranny has come to America in a bland, institutionalized form, without a dynamic and demonic authority figure like Hitler or Mussolini. So how do you think Sheldon, who died in fall 2015, would have accounted for the rise of Trump?***

I asked Wolin about this issue. He argued that the political pacifiers of the unemployed and working poor are cheap consumer products and access to easy credit. This changed after the meltdown of 2008. If these pacifiers disappeared, he conceded, we could devolve into a system that resembles a more classical form of fascism.

*And so the beast with orange hair began slouching toward Bethlehem. And he clearly tapped into the long-simmering rage and resentment of these working families and underclass. And along with this electrifying leader, came all the other hallmarks of classic fascism—the overheated rhetoric, the scapegoating of minorities, the thuggish violence.*

It's what I've been writing about for ten years in books like *American Fascists* and in my last book, *Wages of Rebellion*. The rage is legitimate, but it fosters a retreat into magical thinking. Violence is directed against all who appear to have been empowered at the expense of a disenfranchised white working class—African-Americans, Muslims, undocumented workers, homosexuals, feminists, artists and intellectuals. It is absurd to believe that the persecution of these groups will bring back the old order, but the yearning for a mythological past, one where white supremacy was largely unchallenged and there were good jobs, is so powerful it gives rise to a Christianized fascism. Anthropologists call these crisis cults. This is what the Ghost Dance was about. Wear these magic shirts and they will repel bullets. The white men will disappear. The buffalo herds will return. And the warriors under the earth will rise from the dead.

**In Wages of Rebellion, *I do think you caught the sense of what now seems to be happening with frightening speed in our country. In the book, which came out in spring 2015, you write, "the unraveling of America mirrors the unraveling of Yugoslavia." You saw those terrifying events unfold in the Balkans with your own eyes.***

### In what ways do you think the two situations are similar?

Karl Polanyi observed that fascism, like socialism, is rooted in a market economy that has ceased to function. In the former Yugoslavia you had an ineffectual liberal center that took power after the dictator Tito died. These ineffectual political leaders tried to build, with few resources, a "democratic" Yugoslavia, even though the country had no history of democracy. When the economy collapsed, in part because the West would not renegotiate Yugoslavia's massive loans, this liberal center was impotent and discredited. The economic collapse vomited up the ethnic nationalists, warlords, gangsters and demagogues such as the Serbian leader Slobodan Milosevic, who began the war.

### You also had, in the Balkans, a long history of ethnic and religious rivalries and hatred, right?

I don't buy that theory, promoted by neocons like Robert Kaplan [*Balkan Ghosts*], about ancient ethnic hatreds. Yugoslavs were the East European country best adapted to integrate into Europe. Life in Yugoslavia under Tito, economically, was heaven, compared to the rest of Eastern Europe. Yugoslavs had relatively high wages. Health and education was free. Pensions were good. They traveled freely. There were only four countries in the world where Yugoslavs needed visas.

The economic collapse, which discredited liberal democracy in the eyes of many Yugoslavs, was more important than ancient ethnic hatreds. This was the era of the neoliberal shock doctrine. Massive state factories closed. There was high unemployment and hyperinflation. Rage rippled through the country. Scapegoats were sought. That's when you got "ancient ethnic hatreds."

I was in Montgomery, Alabama with Bryan Stevenson, the great civil rights attorney. We were walking through the city. It was filled with Confederate memorials. Bryan, who was born there, says, "You know, most of these statues and what not went up in the last ten years"—in other words, during the economic decline. And I say, "Bryan, that's just like Yugoslavia, before its crackup." You lose hope and you retreat into a mythic narrative of the glorious and tragic past. It is all you have. That's what these white people in Montgomery did. It is what the Yugoslavs did. It is what the Germans did in Weimar.

### Worshipping a defeated past?

I'm not so sure about "defeated." If you are black in the South you could make a pretty strong argument the Confederacy won the war. Slavery, and the terror and violence that came with it, was perpetuated by another name. Slaves became convicts. But since they were no longer property the abuse was even greater. Their life expectancy plummeted. You had to buy slaves. Convicts were free. Sharecropping. Jim and Jane Crow. Lynching. Slavery is still with us. I teach in a prison where prisoners are lucky to make 22 cents an hour and often make nothing. Meanwhile, as you point out, poor whites romanticize a vanquished past that never existed but that they are determined to recreate.

### "Old times there are not forgotten." But I meant that white Southerners cling to this sense of humiliated heroism—and of course so many Americans, particularly Trump's constituency, feel this same humiliation today.

Collective humiliation does strange things to a society. We see people turning with fury against the elites, who sold them out, along with values that these elites claim to promote. But they are seeking to reclaim their dignity with magical thinking.

### So what you saw unfold in the Balkans might also happen here?

We are not immune. When a society disintegrates, as ours is disintegrating, when you acculturate people to speak in the language of violence, you eventually get violence. I don't know how far it will go. But it will get worse.

### So we now see leaders who play on people's sense of grievance and their fear and ignorance of "the other." And you get this rising volume of hate speech. "These people are taking advantage of us" or "They're out to get us" or "We're not going to take it anymore."

Yes, that's right. For instance, in Belgrade they used to run endless nighttime shows on Serbian television about the Ustasê—the Croatian fascist brigades who murdered thousands of Serbs and Jews during World War II—or about the Muslim SS battalion. The hatred was stoked by mass media. This is the role of Fox News and right-wrong talk radio. A society that allows this hate speech to pollute their airwaves pays for it.

The Serbian leader Milosevic was a technocrat and a banker. But he knew how to touch the right nerve. There's a video of him in Kosovo speaking to ethnic Serbs who were being harassed by the Kosavar Albanian majority. He says, "I will not allow them to beat you." You see the crowd's wild reaction. You see the light turn on in Milosevic. Trump's speeches are the same—he incites, incites, incites. The potential consequences are catastrophic. Catastrophic.

### *A slow-motion nightmare.*

Even in Nazi Germany it was a slow process. In her book *The Nazi Conscience*, Claudia Koonz points out that between 1933 and '38 Hitler only mentions the Jews three times. The Brownshirts engaged in spasms of violence. Hitler would often reprimand them, saying, "Oh, they shouldn't do that." It takes time to deform a society. But that's what's happening, that's what's going on here.

The groundwork for Trump was laid for many years by the Republican Party. It has long exploited racial and religious hatreds, along with homophobia and misogyny. The ground was fertile. The Clintons, but the way, played the same game in their rise to power.

### *Like Sister Souljah and the spooky specter of the "super predator."*

Exactly. Trump didn't create this reign of intolerance. He made it more blatant. He exposed the hypocrisy of the political elites. Right-wing populism is dangerous. It does speak a truth. The rage, as in most proto-fascist movements, is legitimate. Trump attacked free trade as a betrayal of working-class America. This, more than his racism, is what made the elites apoplectic. They don't care about his bashing of minorities, except that it may drive away voters. They don't give a damn about the poor or black and brown people. But all the stuff about NAFTA and the Trans-Pacific treaty…that got the elites where they live. That is how they get rich.

### *So it was Trump's attacks on these global treaties that finally triggered the massive media assault on him, after months of playing up his circus to boost ratings?*

Yes. Of course.

*Knowing, as you do, about the fascist violence of the past, in Germany and Yugoslavia and so on, do you feel that bloodshed is inevitable in this country?*

Something of this magnitude would only occur in the midst of a huge crisis, one caused by the total collapse of the economy, severe effects from climate change, catastrophic acts of domestic terrorism, something of that nature. Once we have system breakdowns, anything is possible.

*Do you think there's a way for Trump's constituency to be won over by the Left? After all, they share many of the same legitimate grievances against the political and financial elites.*

No. Trump does what all fascists do. He blames the vulnerable—Muslims, undocumented workers, feminists, liberals, and intellectuals. It is not a tactic the Left can co-opt.

*Ralph Nader has been arguing for an alliance between the Left and Right against the corporate state.*

I admire Ralph tremendously, but perhaps on this point he's culturally deaf. The same with Noam Chomsky, whom I'm also reluctant to criticize since he's our greatest intellectual. But Nader and Chomsky don't always grasp the irrationality of religion and mass culture.

*On some level, they don't understand human beings, because they're such rational men.*

Perhaps that is the curse of being so brilliant. And they are right that none of this madness makes sense. But that is the point. These people on the far right have migrated to a non-reality based belief system. We will not argue them out of it.

*I assume neither Nader nor Chomsky hangs out a lot with armed and angry people on the right?*

Probably not. In *American Fascists* I conclude that the only way to stop the rise of fascism here is to re-integrate these people economically into the life of the country. Otherwise, we're doomed. The book was written back in 2006. The problem is even more urgent now. When you disempower people, then the only power they feel is embodied in a self-constructed mythology and state violence.

*So you get roars from the Trump crowds at one his favorite speech lines—that we're going to start winning again, that we're going to knock the hell out of ISIS, that no one is going to mess with us anymore.*

Right.

*If not politically, is there a way to win over these angry, disenfranchised people on the right through culture? Barbara Ehrenreich once said that the only thing standing between the American working class and fascism is Bruce Springsteen.*

I admire Bruce Springsteen as an artist and a man with a conscience…

*And he's beloved by a lot of these working people, his songs are filled with their pain.*

But he's also beloved by Chris Christie. That stuff doesn't make any difference. I knew Marine Corps killers who listened to the Grateful Dead. When it comes to this kind of violence, we're not really talking about blue-collar workers. We're talking about the dispossessed underclass. They're not the proletariat. They're the lumpenproletariat. Marx got it. They are always the shock troops of any totalitarian movement.

## *Yes, Hitler got it too...*

Every totalitarian regime understands the violent potential of those cast aside by society. You're not going to convert them through culture. You're not going to convert them by lovely speechmaking or religious sermons. When I covered the Christian Right, I never lied about who I was. I told them my father was a minister and I had graduated from seminary. They never wanted to talk with me about the Bible. They did not know the Bible. All they knew were the biblical clichés they had been fed. They were selective literalists who pulled out from the Bible what supported their ideology.

# VII. The Bankruptcy of the Liberal Elites

*Let me give you a chance to gloat here a little bit. In George Packer's review of your 2015 book* Wages of Rebellion *in the* New York Times, *he ridiculed your assertion that we live in a revolutionary moment. He said that is "not remotely true" and he dismissed your book as an illogical rant. His review, of course, came out a few months before the rise of Trump and the most tumultuous presidential campaign in years, when leading candidates in both parties started calling for a new American revolution. So who described this historical moment best – you or Packer?*

Packer and I clashed publicly in the past, especially over the call to invade Iraq. If he had any integrity he would have refused to accept the review assignment. He is the classic courtier. He was a "liberal" cheerleader for the war in Iraq. When the war went bad he said, "Oh, I was wrong." But he wasn't wrong. He did what all courtiers do. He served his status and his career. These elitist liberals are used to discredit those of us who defy the system and their bankrupt ideology. I don't know what he really believes. I suspect he believes what will best ingratiate him with the powerful.

This is why all those who were wrong about the war, and those who are wrong about what is happening at this moment, still have prominent platforms. It does not matter. The job of someone like Packer is to position himself as a liberal voice in support of official policy. He serves the elites by discrediting their critics on the left. It gets him invited to their dinner parties and social events. They deserve each other.

**Did you respond to his review?**
No.

**Why not?**
I don't see the point. It allows your critics to set the agenda. And I don't see how in a 500 or 600 words letter to the Book Review I am going to make a cogent argument to state my position. It took me 286 pages to do this in the book. I also don't care that much. I stay off social media. I don't Tweet. I don't have a Facebook page. I don't have a web page. I did not like his review. But I also did not lose sleep over it. It was what I expected.

**I don't know—I always liked how Ishmael Reed put it—"writin' is fightin'." If your book gets unfairly attacked in the New York Times, don't you think it's your job as a writer to fight back?**
I fight back by staying focused on what is important. Most of my readers do not care what they write about me in the *New York Times*.

*Well, I wouldn't respond to every critic– that is a waste of energy. But when a big, fat target like George Packer comes at you in the New York Times, then maybe it's time to go to war. I did, when my book Season of the Witch was weirdly and viciously attacked by a woman who had worked for me at Salon, and—like Packer—she failed to inform the Times of her connection to me. And I made an issue of it when the Times and the Washington Post decided to completely ignore my book on the dark side of US intelligence, The Devil's Chessboard—which, among other things, revealed how complicit both newspapers have been with the CIA. It still became a New York Times bestseller, by the way, which of course I took great pleasure in.*

The *Times* trashed my book on the Christian Right and it also made it onto the *New York Times* bestseller list. The paper is not as important as it thinks it is. I should know. I worked there.

*But this turning the other cheek...are you maybe being too Christian?*

Well, I am certainly not an orthodox Christian. I am, as Graham Greene once said, a Christian agnostic. I also have limited amounts of time and energy. I spent many years being attacked, including by the Israeli lobby. I spent five years in Central America being attacked by the Reagan administration. You can't let it eat you up. It comes with the territory. Keep fighting. They may get you in the end. They often do.

*Just keep going forward.*

Exactly.

*By the way, do you read responses from readers?*
Not often.

*So you don't care much about reader feedback either?*
The comments are usually not very illuminating. I don't like anonymous comments. It brings out the trolls.

*And you don't believe in social media?*
It is largely about self-promotion. It feeds the cult of the self. It is an attempt to become in our own tiny social circle a celebrity, to create, as Neal Gabler wrote, "Life: The Movie."

*You're a man unto yourself…By the way, when Packer ridiculed you for predicting America was headed toward revolutionary crisis, you meant not necessarily a socialist revolution, but more likely some kind of radical authoritarianism, right?*
Yes. I made that clear in the book. I do not expect we will all be singing "The Internationale" and holding up banners of Marx and Rosa Luxembourg. We may witness mass recitations of the Pledge of Allegiance and kneeling before the flag and the Christian cross.

*Speaking of Rosa Luxemburg, it's not too far-fetched to think we could have our versions of the Reds fighting with the Brownshirts in the streets.*
The old Left, the Wobblies, the Communists, the anarchists, had those kinds of militants. But this radicalism no longer exists in America. But if we did see a violent militancy from the Left the liberal elites would back the fascists. The Freikorps, the fascist shock troops, were armed and mobilized by the Social Democratic Party, the ruling liberal party.

They used the Freikorps, who fed the ranks of the Nazi Party, against the left-wing Spartacus League and allowed them to massacre hundreds in the streets of Berlin. That's an important point. When capitalism is challenged, the liberals line up with the Brownshirts.

### How is this relevant in terms of today's politics?

Who shut down Occupy? It was Barack Obama in a coordinated federal effort. If there is a powerful social movement on the left, a serious one that is anti-capitalist, it's the liberal class that will make the alliance with the forces of repression, the fascists. That's what always happens. The liberal class empowers the fascists, who then ultimately consume them.

We see this today, in the way that the self-identified liberal establishment deifies the US military. They sacralize our war machine and our "fighting men and women." It's a big mistake. They're flirting with their own destruction.

### Yes, whatever happened to the concept of civilian control of the military? You see this militarization of America throughout our culture today—even at sports events, with the Air Forces planes flying over and the Army recruitment videos playing nonstop on all the stadium screens and the never-ending "honor our troops" ceremonies. Now at baseball games you have to not only stand for the "Star Spangled Banner" before the game, but for "America the Beautiful" in the middle of the game.

Yes. And Hollywood and the mass media is completely militarized…

### Films like American Sniper…

That's something Goebbels would have loved…

### *And* Zero Dark Thirty...

Yes. The CIA got its own film. As Seymour Hersh made clear in his reporting, the story put out about the killing of Osama bin Laden by the Pentagon, a story repeated in *Zero Dark Thirty*, is a lie. There was no courier. The CIA learned of bin Laden's whereabouts from a former senior Pakistani intelligence officer. The Pakistanis knew exactly where he was. They had been holding bin Laden as a prisoner at the Abbottabad compound since 2006. Bin Laden did not resist—he was by this time an invalid. He was shot down in cold blood. There was no burial at sea—indeed the Seals tossed pieces of bin Laden's body parts out of the helicopter as they flew back to Afghanistan.

### *Well, the CIA maintains a big office in Hollywood.*

Oliver Stone told me that after he did *JFK*, they opened one. And of course the military has long worked with Hollywood. You can't use military equipment in a movie unless the Pentagon approves the script. But while the liberal establishment and liberal Hollywood valorizes militarism, the military itself hates these people...

### *Hates their liberal values.*

Yes. I've spent a lot of time with the military. They have contempt for the liberal elite. Here's an example. After the Navy Seal team kills Osama bin Laden, they go to the White House and the first thing Obama asks—which you would never do if you come out of the military culture—is, "Who shot bin Laden?" And of course none of them wants to answer. I read an interview later with one of them and he said, "You know, we all hate this guy."

### *Hate Obama.*

Yeah.

*Have contempt for him.*

Yes.

*Because he's not one of them.*

Right.

*So this is a dangerous mistake on the part of the liberal establishment, to valorize the military culture because…*

Military values are antithetical to democracy.

*It appalled me when I was watching the Republican debates and they'd all say, "When I'm president, I'm going to let the generals run the war, I'm going to leave everything in their hands." So much for our democracy.*

But it's not just the Republicans. It's the same with Obama and Clinton.

*Of course, it's the same with the Democrats, but at least you wouldn't hear a Bernie Sanders saying this.*

You might not hear Bernie say it, but if he had ever made it to the White House, the generals and the arms manufacturers would still run it. These forces have seized the levers of power.

# VIII. How the Pillars of Power Fall

*Let's talk about rank and file soldiers and the police.* You have some provocative observations to make about this thin blue line, or khaki line in Wages of Rebellion—*since in the end, they're all that really stands between the one percent, with all their growing fortune and privileges, and the wretched of the earth. The first line of defense for the elite, you write, is the media and the government bureaucracy. And finally those in power have the clenched fist of the police and the military. You write that a regime's days are finally numbered when these lines of defense begin to melt away —first the intellectual guard, and then the police guard. And you write that you've seen this happen with remarkable speed in some places around the world. Do you see any signs of that in our current situation?*

The anarchist Alexander Berkman wrote about this in his essay "The Idea is the Thing."

### Emma Goldman's lover.

Yes. Berkman argues it is a subterranean, unseen process. He likens it to water boiling in a kettle. People gradually lose faith in ruling ideologies, in our case neoliberalism. As long as those ideas are unchallenged, the private and state institutions are unassailable. But when these ideas are seen as bankrupt, the institutions that buttress the ruling class collapse. The foot soldiers of the elites, the police, the civil service, no longer defend them. I saw this during the revolutions in Eastern Europe. At that point the regime is finished. No revolution is successful unless large sections of the security apparatus defect or refuse to defend the elites. Americans realize they have been stripped of political power, lost most of their civil liberties and are being forced into poverty. The ideas that sustain the corporate state are losing their efficacy.

The Right has retreated into Christian fascism. It celebrates the gun culture. The Left, knocked off balance by state repression in the name of anti-communism, is struggling to rebuild itself. Popular revulsion for the ruling elite, however, is almost universal. It is a question of which ideas will capture the public's imagination. Either way, the system of neoliberalism is doomed, at least ideologically. If it survives it will be purely through increased state repression.

*Along with the growing bankruptcy of the ruling ideology, do you see a growing disenchantment within the military culture? It seems that tensions are rising in the military, with more and more families feeling that their loved ones have been used and thrown away by ruling elites that claim to honor their service but in reality don't give a damn about them.*

All these sentiments also go into feeding fascism. These former marines and soldiers can always join the ranks of the private contractors or Homeland Security—our own version of the Freikorps.

### *Like Academi, which used to be Blackwater.*

Right. The elites are very concerned about unrest. They've laid the groundwork for massive state repression. They need the military to back them up, because they're not confident the police will protect them.

I sued Obama in federal court to block Section 1021 of the National Defense Authorization Act, which overturns the 1878 Posse Comitatus Act. It allows the military to be a domestic police force and to hold people in military detention centers indefinitely without due process. We won in the Southern District Court of New York. The Obama administration appealed the ruling. It was an amazing, two-year legal and political battle. Our lawyers, Bruce Afran and Carl Mayer, went to [Democratic Congressional leader] Nancy Pelosi. They said, "Just insert some language in the bill, write in there that this does not apply to US citizens and we will drop the law suit." But the Congress didn't write it in, because it *was* written for US citizens.

I was arrested in front of the White House with 133 others, mostly veterans, protesting the wars in Iraq and Afghanistan. Most of the cops were in the National Guard. They had been to Iraq and Afghanistan. They would whisper to us, "Keep protesting." When I was arrested with 100 others during Democracy Spring in front of the Capital to protest the capture of our political system by corporate money, the cops asked us as they escorted us away, "How do we get money out of politics?" When Chicago teachers marched through the streets of Chicago, they used the bathrooms in the precinct houses. The cops would applaud them. This terrifies the elites.

### You saw some of that with New York City cops at Zuccotti Park too, right?

The demeanor of the blue uniformed police changed abruptly when the white shirts, their officers, appeared. There was a lot of fraternization between the protesters and the blue shirts when the white shirts weren't around. Most of the worst physical assaults on the protesters were carried out by the white shirts. We held teach-ins—it was like the '60s. I held a teach-in once—everybody's sitting on the concrete –and two cops stood on the edge of the crowd listening. When I finished, the cops came up to me and one said, "Could you send us a copy of your book?" Which I did.

I don't want to romanticize the police, especially given the lethal force they use indiscriminately in poor neighborhoods of color, but there are some we can reach. And it is vital we reach them. I gave a talk at Occupy once criticizing the Black Bloc anarchists for taunting the police. They weren't very significant at Zuccotti.

### More so in Occupy Oakland.

Yes. They effectively sabotaged the Oakland Occupy movement. I have always suspected they were very heavily infiltrated by police and Homeland Security who used the Black Bloc to demonize Occupy. I said, "These blue uniform police have to spend all day long with these white-shirted assholes, but we only have to deal with the white shirts an hour or two a day." It goes out on YouTube. A few months after they shut down Occupy, I give a talk in New York. This guy comes up to me and says, "I'm a white-shirted asshole and I read your books." He may be the only one. But it was a good lesson. I should not have insulted even the white shirts.

So anyway, that's why, when I've given talks to conservative audiences, I always dress in a business suit with a white, buttoned-down shirt and tie. I learned that from Ralph Nader and Sy Hersh. I have establishment credentials. I was vetted and rewarded by the establishment. This gives me a status that other radicals such as Norman Finkelstein lack. He began fighting the Israeli lobby in graduate school and they prevented him from ever being embraced by the establishment. But I come out of...

### ...the hated liberal elite...

Yes, and when people in the audience ask me if I still work for the *New York Times,* I tell them, "You haven't heard a thing I said if you think I still work there." And I think that resonates with a lot of people who aren't on the left.

*I want to go back to the* **Times** *review of* **Wages of Rebellion,** *and the general way that your work has been ignored or marginalized or ridiculed by the mainstream media—which is, of course, the central theme of this new series, "Unspeakable." You've gotten this treatment despite the high quality and importance of your reporting and writing. And, of course, you have a large and respectful following – but that seems to have no sway with the media gatekeepers. Of course, you're not alone – other public intellectuals who disturb the mainstream narrative like Chomsky and Cornel West have* *also been blacked out. But occasionally a radical truth-teller does break through and suddenly starts appearing on TV—like Glenn Greenwald, my old colleague at Salon, did—particularly after the Edward Snowden story broke. Why is someone like Greenwald an exception to this media blackout?*

Because Glenn is taking on the security and surveillance state, which huge parts of the establishment don't like. That's why Pierre Omidyar [the billionaire founder of eBay] is funding Greenwald's online enterprise, *The Intercept*. Omidyar might have criticisms of the national security state, as a libertarian and technology entrepreneur—but, as far as I can tell, he really wasn't interested in taking on Wall Street, and that's why he got rid of [muckraking financial reporter] Matt Taibbi. I don't want to take anything away from Glenn – whom I admire and respect and like and read—but his focus is different and doesn't threaten financial power the way Taibbi did, so therefore his critique is palatable.

I suspect Omidyar hired Taibbi because he writes with biting humor. But I imagine he didn't really want Taibbi to take down Wall Street. And Matt's a serious guy, he exposes the crimes of Wall Street, which he does really well. *Griftopia* is a very fine book. But they don't appear interested in that confrontation.

Like I said, this is not a knock on Glenn –he's a constitutional lawyer, that's his expertise, that's what he cares about. I think Glenn followed his passion, his integrity, and did what he did what he wanted to do—exposing the security and surveillance empire. But that was a critique that, within fairly large segments of the power elite, was acceptable. But people like Chomsky and me have critiques that are more broad—we go far beyond the security and surveillance state.

*As does Glenn—he's written on a variety of topics, including a book about our class-based system of justice [With Liberty and Justice for Some]. But you're right, what primarily got him on TV was his defense of Snowden.*

Yeah, you can see that they'll pick and choose. For instance, Joe Sacco, whom I admire a lot and have worked with—Joe wrote one of the great books on Israel and Palestine, a graphic novel called *Footnotes in Gaza*. But he couldn't get any play on that book, and it's brilliant. Then he does a book on World War I and suddenly he's on NPR, he's all over the place. I mean they pick and choose when to spotlight you.

*I want to go back to the Occupy movement. You clearly think that was a significant turning point...*

Occupy gave people the language of the wealth gap that we're hearing all around us now, and that's not small. That whole language of the 1 percent came out of Occupy.

*I was at Zuccotti that first weekend of Occupy Wall Street...*

I was there too.

*I filed one of the first articles about it, for Salon. And I was enthralled by it—and how it spread to other cities like San Francisco, where I live, and Oakland. And for me, as I walked through these camps and talked with people, I found the whole idea of horizontal instead of top-down leadership thrilling, because they were avoiding a lot of the mistakes made by the New Left and the antiwar movement of my generation...the hierarchies, the sexism, and so on. But, on the other hand, because Occupy was so fundamentally anti-organization, or at least traditional organization, it also turned out to be a fleeting phenomenon. In other words, they made a lot of their own mistakes...*

But that's all right, because they learned from those mistakes.

*I know you are some version of an anarchist, but to me the age-old problem with anarchism is how do you sustain a movement if you don't have structure and leadership?*

You don't. All movements have leaders. Occupy had leaders. They stayed, however, in the background. There were two dynamics that destroyed the Occupy movement. One dynamic is that it internally combusted. The second dynamic is that it was infiltrated and shut down.

After losing Zuccotti, there was an attempt to occupy Duarte Square, which was property owned by Trinity Church in lower Manhattan. Duarte Square had cyclone fencing with entrances and exits. It would have allowed the movement to control who came in and out. It would have brought order to what became chaos.

The security state realized it could overload the Occupy system. They were dropping homeless people off at the park. Prisoners being released from Rikers were taken to Zuccotti. With the colder weather came individual tents. That's when the drugs appeared and we saw sexual assaults. Activists were staying up all night in de-escalation teams rather than organizing.

*So by the time they were contemplating the Duarte action, their structure was starting to evolve?*

They were never able to take Duarte Square. But they had learned.

I was there a lot. I was interviewed a lot about it. But I always spoke about them in the third person. I had a lot of trouble with people, many of them celebrities, who would come down and use the camp as a backdrop for interviews and then disappear.

The Occupy movement was very moving. It was a public manifestation of what I had been writing about and calling for—ground-level resistance. I never told people how to resist. I only knew we had to resist. I learned a lot from these activists. They were amazing men and women.

## How did you support Occupy?

Various ways. I wrote press releases. I spent a lot of time there. Cornel West and I had a people's hearing on Goldman Sachs. I was arrested in front of Goldman Sachs. I did teach-ins. I marched in the streets. I would speak. But they key word is support. It was their movement. I did not organize it.

At one point, after Mayor Bloomberg tried to shut down the park and failed, we knew they were going to make another, stronger attempt. Some members of the direct action committee came to my house in Princeton. They camped out on the floor—which thrilled my kids. This was pre-Snowden. They knew, however, they were under surveillance. They wanted to discuss possible tactics—namely how they were going to resist when Bloomberg's police raided the park. So for security purposes, as we met at my house, they put all their electronics in my car in the driveway. No one spoke. They wrote ideas on pieces of paper. We then burned them in my fireplace.

It was decided that about 20 activists would chain themselves to the camp kitchen when the cops hit the park. The kitchen was in the center of the park. When the raid took place, the police got to the kitchen and did not have chain cutters. It took four hours to get them. It was a message to the police—you do not know everything. It was a Pyrrhic victory.

### Do you think the Black Lives Matter movement learned from Occupy?

Yes, clearly. People who came out of Occupy are taking roles in Black Lives Matter and other types of resistance, such as the anti-fracking movement and the drive to raise the minimum wage. Maybe we should look at Occupy as a tactic rather than a movement, the way that Rosa Parks remaining in her seat on the bus was a tactic and the Freedom Rides were a tactic. Did they make mistakes? Of course, but they did a hell of a lot more than the rest of us have done. I admire them.

### Like you say, it changed the political language...

It empowered a lot of people. It gave them a sense of community they didn't have before. It gave them a language to explain their reality.

### Do we need a new theory of revolution today? One that replaces the old Marxist-Leninist concept of smashing the state with a less explosive vision of radical change? That's what the neo-Marxist scholar John Holloway among others argues. His revolutionary model envisions a system of cracks in the capitalist system throughout the world, an Occupy or Black Lives here, and similar liberation efforts in Spain and Mexico and Greece, as you mentioned earlier...various blows to the system of global capitalism that finally de-legitimize it and bring it down. What do you think about that?

Holloway is right. We need a vision that unites all these groups. This has happened in Spain and Greece. There are severe cracks in the system. There is a loss of faith in the ruling ideology, even among many of the elites.

The historian Crane Brinton in his book *Anatomy of a Revolution* laid out the prerequisites for revolution. These include discontent that affects nearly all social classes, widespread feelings of entrapment and despair, unfulfilled expectations, a unified solidarity in opposition to a tiny power elite, a refusal by scholars and thinkers to continue to defend the actions of the ruling class, an inability of government to respond to the basic needs of citizens, a steady loss of will within the power elite itself and defections from the inner circle, a crippling isolation that leaves the power elite without any allies or outside support and, finally, a crisis, usually economic. Our corporate elite has amply fulfilled these preconditions. But it is Brinton's next observation that is most important. Revolutions always begin, he wrote, by making impossible demands that if the government met would mean the end of the old configurations of power, such as wresting back power from corporations. The second stage, the one we have entered now, is the unsuccessful attempt by the power elite to quell the unrest and discontent through physical acts of repression. The vast internal security and surveillance machine is not primarily about fighting terrorism but about keeping us contained.

The tipping point is always the same. In revolutionary Russia, for instance, what was the tipping point that led to the abdication of the Czar? It was the bread riots in Petrograd and the Cossacks refusing to fire on the crowd. What was it that terminated the regime in Iran? It was the announcement the Shah had fled and the armed forces would no longer fight to defend the regime. Same in Cuba. Even in the French Revolution, what was the tipping point? It's when the armed forces would no longer defend Louis XVI and defected to the revolutionaries. I watched this in 1989 in Eastern Europe. When the foot soldiers of the elite—the police, the army, the civil service—no longer defend a discredited system. And when that happens, no matter what the resources of that regime, the regime is finished.

*This concept of withdrawing support from the regime and allowing it to fall reminds me of the French political theorist Etienne de la Boetie, who was a close friend and intellectual partner of Montaigne. He writes that we don't have to put our hands violently on those in power, to make a revolution—we simply have to withdraw our hands and stop supporting the power structure. And the moment we do that, the structure falls. That's a beautiful concept. Of course, Boetie is writing this is in the 1500s, long before the bloodshed of the French Revolution.*

That's right. That is exactly it. As the Communist regime was teetering on the brink, the East German dictator [Erich] Honecker sends an elite paratroop division to Leipzig to fire on the crowd. The local Communist Party officials in Leipzig say, "Absolutely not!" Honecker is out of power within a week. The same was true in the Velvet Revolution—and I was there—when the police and the armed authorities in Czechoslovakia wouldn't fire on the crowd. At that moment, it's over. And the house of cards, which days before looked unassailable, topples with dizzying speed.

*What did it feel like to cover that historic moment in Eastern Europe, as the Iron Curtain fell?*

It happens so fast, it's hard to wrap your head around it. It was a kind of Alice in Wonderland feeling. After

Honecker was gone, the ruling party desperately tried to offer one reform after another, not realizing that it had become irrelevant. It was hard keeping track of who was in power. And then it was all over. Suddenly you could walk through the abandoned Communist Party building in East Berlin that had always been off limits to nonparty members.

***It must be so startling, so overwhelming for people in those societies, when such an iron structure disappears so quickly.***
Well, when you look back you see all the cracks and fissures, but because the superstructure is still standing you don't know how corroded it is until it collapses.

***Rotting slowly from within. And you think it's true, here in America, the same process of decay has been underway for some time in the ruling order?***
Yes. But these decaying regimes can be a lot more resilient than you expect. It took the Ottoman Empire a century of decay to finally collapse. The Austro-Hungarian Empire was already dead, from 1850 on, before World War I made it official.

***But the cadaver keeps stumbling forward...***
That's a good analogy...it was a completely ossified, dysfunctional system, the walking dead.

***And when these dying systems finally do fall...***
Well, if you have not articulated an alternative vision, then what happens is chaos, which isn't a revolution. Chaos without a revolutionary vision is easily crushed. The elites can handle chaos.

*This kind of chaos emboldened the rising fascist forces in Germany, for instance. So how do you have coordination in a revolutionary moment without having a vanguard elite, the Leninist concept of revolution that ends up stifling the popular will?*

That is the fundamental question. I do not have a glib answer. As repression mounts, the need for a vanguard elite becomes more important because it is so difficult to resist openly.

*Have we ever seen revolutionary change take place in history, without the leadership of a revolutionary elite?*

Sure. There was no real coordination in East Germany. It was just a spontaneous uprising.

*Yes, but the fall of the Berlin Wall, as liberating as that was, didn't produce a revolutionary society in Germany—it simply incorporated East Germany into a democratic capitalist state via a unified Germany.*

The leaders of the revolution in East Germany wanted to create a democratic socialism—but once that wall fell and everybody in the east went over and started looking at the chic store windows on the Kurfürstendamm, it was over. The problem in Eastern Europe was they didn't understand the insidious dynamics of capitalism. This was Pope John Paul II's blindness too. They didn't understand the evils of capitalism. They conflated democracy with capitalism. Capitalism and democracy are ultimately incompatible.

Of course, many revolutions become counter-revolutions. Look at the French Revolution under Napoleon, who said, "I am the revolution." Lenin seized power with armed paramilitary units, destroying the autonomous soviets, banning opposition parties, censoring the press, creating the secret police and forming centralized state capitalism.

### And the Arab Spring.

Yes, look at Egypt. After the uprising Tahrir Square uprising in 2011, the military abandoned Mubarak and supported elections. But it then overthrew the elected president, Mohamed Morsi, and established a military regime more vicious than the one run by Mubarak.

*I want to bring up another possible revolutionary model. In* **Wages of Rebellion,** *you also quote Thomas Linzey, a leader of the community rights movement. I have heard him speak and find his model for change inspiring—this model of local resistance to state and corporate power, particularly when it comes to defending a community's environmental and public health.*

Community resistance is all well and good. But you can't simply do what the Zapatistas in Mexico did, which was to create these local, liberated—or "snail"—zones. We have to overthrow centralized power. The Mexican federal government is the problem. It is selling off national assets like the Pemex oil company. It is cutting Mexican social programs. There's a lot of dialogue between radical Mexican activists and the Zapatistas about the limits of the Zapatista strategy. There is a growing understanding that these autonomous zones helped build political consciousness in Mexico, but if they stop there, they're not going to seriously disrupt the system. If they remain isolated, they'll always be vulnerable to government repression, so at a later date they can always be wiped out.

*But don't you think someone like Linzey understands that, as he analyzes how power works in this country? He seems to get that community rebellions need to link up and form a national resistance movement against the corporate despoiling of communities.*

Linzey understands that the problem is democracy. He understands that by building local movements we can create a model of what real democracy looks and feels like. That is a good place to start. But it has to ultimately go beyond this, as I think Linzey would probably agree.

*It's not enough to simply act locally, even if you're thinking globally. You have to go beyond that.*

Right. An autonomous zone within an antagonistic corporate capitalist state has a terminal life span, unless it directly takes on the state.

*So I want to get a little more clear about one of the strategies you advocate in* Wages. *You put forward this idea of withdrawing from the capitalist system, by creating alternative systems of production and governance. But essentially that's what the Left in Greece tried to do, the Syriza Party, as a way out of the terrible corner that the country had been forced into by the European Union and European bankers. They tried to rebel against the shackles of global capitalism, but unfortunately—as the plight of the Greek people grew more desperate—Syriza Party leader Alex Tsipras caved to the enormous pressure and felt compelled to accept the EU's conditions for a deal...So is it ever really possible to secede from global capital?*

It's true. The European financial and political elites told the Syriza Party they would, in essence, do what the US did to

[President Salvador] Allende in Chile—fuel shortages, food shortages, equipment shortages, the disappearance of medicines and other essential supplies. Greece is economically tied to Europe. It imports, hundreds of tons of fresh produce a year. Its pharmaceuticals come from Europe. The bankers are determined to use this dependency to teach Greece a lesson. This has nothing to do with economics. It is a political war. They can't let this kind of rebellion happen in Greece. Spain or Ireland may be next. They made it clear they would destroy Greece. So Syriza caved. Tspiras did not want to cope with that level of human misery and suffering.

**So how do you secede from a system like global capitalism without provoking this massive counter reaction that makes life for the people utterly intolerable?**
That's a very good question. They will not make it easy.

**Especially since financial systems and various production systems—agriculture, technology, manufacturing—are increasingly centralized and integrated into a global capitalist order. Taking on this global power as a beleaguered nation seems extremely daunting.**
Absolutely.

**It seems that building an effective resistance to a very cohesive system of global capital requires the same sort of coordination, between labor, environmental and consumer groups in various countries. Do you see signs of this as you look around the world?**
Movements in Latin America and in European countries like in Greece and Spain understand we're engaged in a global

fight against corporate capitalism. It's not a consciousness we always have. This is one of my problems with the Bernie Sanders Left. We can't be worried about political expedience, we have to unite with *all* of the world's oppressed. We can't – especially those of us who are Americans –decide who among the oppressed is going to be convenient, politically, to support. We have to stand with all those around who are being victimized and exploited. It is the same fight. And we will only win it when we fight together.

### All the "unpeople"—to use Chomsky's term for how the US government treats victim populations around the world.

There is much that the American people have to learn from those who are resisting this dehumanizing treatment around the world. Occupy learned a lot from the Spanish *indignados* – but, in general, our political consciousness is low. Mexican activists are way ahead of us. The Zapatistas formed the day NAFTA was signed in 1993. Most Americans didn't at first get NAFTA when Bill Clinton rammed it through. But the Zapatistas got it.

# IX. The Isolation of the Independent Intellectual

*Are there any political theorists living today who you are lighting the way for Americans who want to learn?*

Chomsky. Tariq Ali. Arundhati Roy. Angela Davis. Cornel West. Michael Hudson. Rick Wolff. Prabhat Patnaik. And those we recently lost—Howard Zinn and Sheldon Wolin.

*Of course, Chomsky's been completely disappeared by the* New York Times, *despite his enormous intellectual contributions.*

The story was that Abe Rosenthal, who used the paper to deify wealth and placate the elites, had a rule when he was running the *Times* that Chomsky's name could not appear in the newspaper. It wasn't written down but I suspect that it's true.

*Well, Rosenthal has been gone for a long time, but that rule still seems to prevail.*

They did review the recent documentary about Chomsky [*Requiem for the American Dream*]. I rely a lot on writers such as C. Wright Mills and some of the other intellectuals from the '50s—like Jane Jacobs, David Reisman and Dwight Macdonald. Our intellectual class today is very anemic. They've withdrawn into the arcane world of academia. Of course it's very hard to financially sustain yourself as a so-called "public intellectual," to use a term I don't like.

*That's why you're an anomaly.*

Sadly.

*Even though you live in the town of Princeton, you aren't connected to the university, you're not on the faculty?*

I have had two visiting professorships at Princeton. I depend on the library. I can't write my books without access to a good research library.

*But for the most part you're on your own?*

Yes. Living without an academic safety net, and having a family, it's not always pleasant.

*You haven't been tempted to come in from the cold and take a university position?*

Can you see me getting through a tenure committee?

*With all the corporate endowments and administrative pressures, it's another system of thought control.*

Completely.

*I have to say that the left-wing press in this country, where I've spent my entire life, has also not been able to produce and sustain many important journalists. When I look at progressive media in my lifetime, and our apparent inability to have a major impact on public consciousness or seriously change the national conversation, I get a little depressed.*

Yes. This is by design. And those very few institutions that once gave a voice to those outside of the mainstream have atrophied. In the 1960s, you could turn on PBS and see Malcolm X. You could see Noam Chomsky and James Baldwin. The argument for public broadcasting is that it exists to permit voices that are not managed or approved by the power elites to be heard. It should be a sanctuary for serious thought and serious culture. NPR and PBS, dependent on corporate sponsorship, have been destroyed as independent platforms. And this has impoverished our national debate.

*You could even see Gore Vidal on network talk shows in those days, on* **The Dick Cavett Show** *and* **Johnny Carson** *and so on...*

Yes, Gore Vidal broke into mainstream network TV, but...

*He was a master showman...*

Exactly. We could never say this about Chomsky. He has always prided himself on *not* being entertaining.

*I think NPR is a vast repository of safe and banal thought. How often do their programs feature truly challenging thinkers or political dissidents? It reeks of Beltway conventional wisdom.*

Yes. I can hardly listen to it. On the tenth anniversary of the war, *Morning Edition* interviewed [former Bush administration official] Paul Wolfowitz reverentially. It was unbelievable.

### *Not putting him on the spot at all...*
No, no, very insipid—"What do you think we've learned?" and so on. The parameters of acceptable debate in this country have narrowed—as Dorothy Parker once said of Katharine Hepburn's emotional range as an actress—from A to B. Step outside of those parameters and you are in the wilderness.

### *I take it you weren't asked by national TV or radio shows to comment on the war during the tenth anniversary?*
No, and I know what I am talking about. I spent seven years in the Middle East, four of them as the Middle East bureau chief for the *Times*. I spent months in Iraq. I speak Arabic. But I don't parrot the dominant narrative.

### *Speaking of the neoconservatives who pushed us into war in Iraq, like Wolfowitz, William Kristol, Robert Kagan, Richard Perle and all those guys in Cheney's shop—how did someone from the left like Christopher Hitchens get wrapped up with them?*
The problem with those who come from a rigid ideological tradition like Hitchens is that you can you swing from one extreme side to the other in an instant. I did not have much respect for Hitchens. He was amoral. It was always about him. He was basically a bully...

### *And yet he continues to wield influence, even from the grave. They keep bringing out his books of essays and paying homage to him. I knew Chris. I think*

*I published one of his first stories in America, in Mother Jones, soon after he came over to the US— ironically, it was a take-down on Tom Wolfe and his fashionably insulting neoconservatism. Watching Chris's political evolution—or devolution—over the years, I assumed that a lot of it had to do with his heavy drinking. Alcoholics don't always have the best sense of judgment.*

No, you know what it was? Fear. When 9/11 happened, guys like him shit in their pants.

### Fear of what?

Fear of terrorism. Fear of Islam. He wanted the 101rst Airborne to protect him. He was spineless—bullies often are.

*Not to mention ignorant. Of course Hitchens presented himself as fearless, as someone like Orwell who was willing to speak tough truths, even to his friends on the left.*

He had a lot more of Hemingway in him than Orwell.

### Where would that fear come from in someone like Chris—do you have any sense?

It's always the big talkers, the guys who strut through the hotel dining hall like they're John Wayne that are the first to crumble when the bombs go off.

### Did he cover wars?

He never covered war. He wasn't anywhere near war. I did it as a job. It's the people who don't talk, the quiet ones, who are real. I did an event with Norman Mailer once on war. He and I were on the stage. He was talking as if we're the only real men in the room. I thought to myself, "This does not sound like somebody who's been in combat." If you've been in combat, if you've tasted that much of your own fear...

### But Mailer served in the Pacific during World War II...

He was a cook. I read it in his obituary. I like *The Naked and the Dead*. I took it with me to our event. But I thought he was such an asshole, I didn't ask him to sign it. He and Hitchens had the same kind of swagger. But people who really go through war, you don't come out like that.

### Hitchens came out of a military family—his father was a commander in the Royal Navy, he sailed the seas for the British Empire. I've wondered how much of the imperial bully that came out in Chris after 9/11 was in there all along, just waiting to flower.

He was an unhappy, amoral human being. He had a terrible relationship with his father. His mother ran off with her lover and committed suicide in a hotel room. He spent his life spewing his venom at the world. I didn't like him even when he was on the left. I didn't trust him.

### You once debated him on stage.

At Berkeley. But it wasn't really a debate. He interrupted me, which is a standard tactic on the right to avoid a debate. He mischaracterized what I said. When it was my turn to speak, he'd start chanting, "Shame on you for defending suicide bombers"—that kind of bullshit. I was furious. He would mischaracterize my ideas to set up straw men to attack. He could only debate this cartoon version of religion. He didn't know anything about religion. He knew only his fundamentalist cartoon image of Islam or Christianity, like Sam Harris. I had written a book called *American Fascists: The Christian Right and the War on America.* I could hardly be accused of defending this brand of belief. I do not like religious institutions. But Hitchens, like Richard Dawkins or Sam Harris, cannot discuss any of the great theologians like Reinhold Niebuhr, Paul Tillich, Karl Barth or James Cone, because they've never read their work.

### What do you think is behind the rise of these new atheists like Harris and Dawkins?

They're secular fundamentalists. Chomsky calls them religious fanatics—for the state religion. I've debated people on the Christian Right. Debating the so-called new atheists is like debating the Christian Right. When I debate fundamentalist Christians, they attack me as a secular humanist. It was the same with Hitchens and Harris. They attack you with slogans, instead of ideas. In my debate with Harris, he concluded by saying, "I feel like it's the 15th century and we're debating magic and witches." I don't believe in magic and witches. I don't even argue that Christ was a real historical figure. I don't believe in heaven or hell. They, like all fundamentalists, have a binary, stunted, idiotic worldview. Fundamentalism is about being stupid—Harris is proof of that.

### You've actually been very critical of organized religion.

It has done a lot of evil in the name of religion.

### But at the same time, you see the liberating or transforming possibilities of faith?

God is a human concept, a way every culture attempts to name the non-rational forces that go into making a complete human being—beauty, grief, love, death, the search for meaning. Jung had chiseled above his doorway, "Called or not, the gods will come." We all have gods. We all worship something – it's what Tillich called "the ultimate concern." It can be money, power, status. We are all easily seduced by idols.

### Who are your gods—or what is your god?

Daniel Berrigan [Catholic priest and activist] defined faith as the belief that the good draws to it the good. Even if all the empirical evidence around you says otherwise—it is that belief in the power of the good. It is a belief in the sanctity of the non-rational. It is a belief that resistance and rebellion are a moral imperative, even if you're doomed to fail. It's not accidental that I'm married to an artist. Art is about grappling with the transcendent. It's why I read a lot of fiction. Art grapples with what people who are authentically religious grapple with. Art and religion, when religions began, were one entity. Religious belief is an imperfect doctrine, a flawed attempt to understand mystery, the ineffable. But the force of life, what Freud called Eros, is real. We live in an age when the forces of death are ascendant. Belief is about affirming life no matter what the cost.

One of the things that happens when a society dies, it destroys its own culture. It loses its capacity to honor and speak of the sacred. It becomes unconscious. It is unable to ask self-critical questions. It engages in an endless and fatal veneration of itself. That's what we've done. In the media. In the universities. In film. On television and radio. Where is the great theater today?

### Where the gods once spoke to the Greek people.

Exactly, where the Greeks were warned about the lethal danger of hubris and how to lead the moral life in the face of inevitable *fortuna*. Where is our contemporary Eugene O'Neill? Our Tennessee Williams? Our Arthur Miller? Our Lorraine Hansberry? Our August Wilson? These are the voices that connect us with our ancestors, if we really want to talk about the true power of theater. We still have some great playwrights—Edward Albee, Sarah Ruhl, Tarell Alvin McCraney and Tony Kushner. But most of theater produced today, like the rest of our cultural landscape, is Disneyfied junk.

There has been a near virtual disappearance of dissident and artistically critical voices. Alexis de Toqueville warned that when democratic populism collapses, when it no longer permits its citizens to engage in a meaningful way politically, it is replaced by an empty cultural populism. This cultural populism, he said, is characterized by the trivial—a bland uniformity, expressions of bitterness and resentment and a mindless patriotism. He called this democratic despotism. It is a world of depoliticized citizens hermetically sealed inside a banal cultural and intellectual vacuum.

*To me, faith– whether it's religious or political belief—is a force that seeks to take us to a higher level, above our own groveling self-interest.*

Yes, when it's good, that's what religion does. Theologian H. Richard Niebuhr [Reinhold's brother] had a great line: religion's a good thing for good people, and a bad thing for bad people. Religion is often misused, as the history of the Catholic Church has evidenced. And I'm going back to the thousand year reign it imposed on Europe, not just the recent pedophilia scandals. Institutions are always the problem. You have to separate the institution from the religious impulse, which must often defy the institution.

**You've written, quoting Reinhold Niebuhr, that it takes a "sublime madness of the soul" to fight against the "malignant powers of the world." If not faith, what gives people the strength of will to fight against seemingly insurmountable problems?**
Faith is indeed a type of madness. There is nothing that's going to rationally justify it. You can know that everything around you points to the fact that your struggle for justice, maybe your entire life, has been futile. But this knowledge doesn't invalidate what you've done.

Rebels are possessed by this "sublime madness." Niebuhr wrote that in moments of extremity "nothing but madness will do battle with malignant power and spiritual wickedness in high places." Without it, as Niebuhr said, "truth is obscured." Liberalism in a crisis he points out is a useless force. It lacks, as Niebuhr said, "the spirit of enthusiasm, not to say, fanaticism, which is so necessary to move the world out of its beaten tracks. It is too intellectual and too little emotional to be an efficient force in history."

There were posters throughout Prague during the Velvet Revolution of Jan Palach, the Charles University student who burned himself alive in Wenceslas Square to protest the 1968 Soviet invasion of Czechoslovakia. The security forces broke up his funeral. It was a non-event, never reported by the state media. When his grave became a shrine, the authorities had his body exhumed. They cremated his remains, and gave them to his mother. She was forbidden from burying them. Palach's martyrdom, it would seem, was lost to history. But two weeks after the Communist government fell in 1989, 10,000 people marched to Red Army Square and renamed it Jan Palach Square.

That is the moral power of resistance. Acts of courage and sacrifice can be written at the time off as useless, but they have a life force that cannot be denied.

Marta Kubisova, the great singer who sang "Prayer for Marta," the anthem of defiance as the Soviet tanks are rolling into Prague in 1968— she was banned from the airwaves, had her recording stock destroyed and was sent to work at an assembly line in a toy factory. But I was there in December 1989 when she walked out on the balcony overlooking Wenceslas Square and began to sing "A Prayer for Marta." There were 500,000 Czechs there. They knew every word.

***But what if you're a revolutionary intellectual like Tom Paine, who helps to make history in America and France—only to end up forgotten by the time he dies, with six people at his funeral? You don't care if that's your fate?***
I don't care.

***Really, you don't care?***
No. If you care, you're in trouble. You cater to the crowd. This is what it means to be possessed by "sublime madness," which Paine certainly was. So was Orwell. And so was Baldwin.

***But adulation aside, don't you think it's important for radical intellectuals and writers to try to make an impact on the public? I've always been frustrated with the ineffectuality of the Left, and its cult of what Leonard Cohen called "beautiful losers"—the notion that you are somehow purer in your failure. I think it's the duty of the writer and the activist to ask themselves, "Am I breaking through in some***

113

UNSPEAKABLE

*way to the public—and if not, why not?" Do you agree with that?*

If you measure your success by your impact and you feel you have a significant impact, then you will easily be seduced into re-configuring what you do. Dwight Macdonald wrote about this in his essay, "Masscult and Midcult." Obviously, I want to have an impact. But I don't want to cater to the wider culture. I won't speak in ways that they dictate. At that point I become like them. And given that choice, it is better to reach a smaller but far more astute and intellectually curious audience.

*So it doesn't bother you, the way you've been marginalized in this country by the mainstream media?*

No. You have to hold fast to your integrity. I am shut out for a reason.

*And that doesn't bother you?*

No.

*Even if—like Orwell and Paine—you're often annoying and outraging the people who brought you to the party, the people who read your books and come hear you speak.*

Who is it we are supposed to emulate in the Christian church? A man who was turned on by the mob, betrayed by all his friends, and executed by the state. So when it comes to writers, Paine is for me the example of the moral life. My goal is to live the moral life. It's not to be a success.

Orwell once wrote about the difference between writers and newspaper reporters. Reporters often don't have the ego of the writers. War correspondents—because the work is so dangerous—are not usually prima donnas. If you take yourself

114

that seriously, you're not going to put yourself in that kind of risk. I don't take myself that seriously. When you're around that much death, you are aware of how finite and insignificant life is. You're more in touch with your tiny place in the universe.

*But I'm thinking of someone like Ed Snowden – he doesn't strike me as someone with a big ego. In fact he seems rather modest and down-to-earth for someone who chose to throw himself into the center of the national security debate. But he said that his greatest fear in overturning his life this way was that it would amount to nothing. That his sacrificial act would be greeted by a giant, collective yawn. So making an impact was clearly important to him. Don't you think it is valid, on some level, if you are going to take that big of a risk, to want to have an impact, to be effective? Certainly as a writer you took calculated risks with your career, even your life.*

Yes. But you should take it even if it does not have an immediate impact. When I covered the war in Kosovo, we knew from readership surveys carried out by the *Times*, that our readers had Balkans fatigue. Only ten percent of the readership was reading what I was writing in Kosovo. And, as you say, my work was dangerous.

*But you still kept doing it.*

I could not get caught up in worrying about the fact that most people weren't reading it.

*Is there a kind of a religious-like commitment to the craft, and to telling the truth for its own sake?*

115

It is about empathy. When you are around that kind of suffering, you feel a commitment to those who are being persecuted. You want to get their story out.

### You are bearing witness?

Yes—because no one else is, or very few people are.

# X. Crime and Punishment

---

*Speaking of suffering and caring, I want to talk about your experience teaching in prison. Being poor is a crime in America, you've written. Whether or not you receive fair and just treatment in our system, of course, depends on your race and your class. What have you learned from teaching inside prison?*

I teach students who care deeply about the life of the mind. They are often very, very bright. They've never had a chance. They're not learning for their career. Most of them won't have a career. They know what's going to happen when they get out, carrying a felony conviction and being black and poor. But when they walk into that classroom, it's the only time in the day when they're treated like human beings. Of course the other prisoners can treat them like human beings, but I mean treated respectfully.

Most people sitting in the prison, 94 percent of them, never had a trial. They were forced to plea out. Usually the ones with the longest sentences are the ones who tried to make the system work. These are the ones who usually didn't commit the crime and who demanded a trial.

***Of course, when they go to trial, they can't afford private attorneys and get stuck with overworked public defenders.***

Right. And so when they're found guilty, they're the ones who get the stiffest sentences. They're being punished for demanding a trial—because if everybody went to trial, the system would crash. It's just an estimate, but maybe 20 or 25 percent of my students did not commit the crime for which they're incarcerated—and I've got guys in there for life. More important, whatever they did, almost none of them had a fair trial, which means the system has condemned them unjustly.

***How often do you teach?***

Twice a week.

***What prison?***

Different prisons. Right now I teach in East Jersey State [originally called Rahway State Prison]. My students get college credit through Rutgers. I taught Chekov in the super-max prison in Trenton last semester.

***What was that like?***

A super-max prison is a terrible place. These people have these horrendous sentences, most know they'll die in prison. There's not a lot of movement allowed in a super-max prison – unlike at East Jersey State, which is a maximum security—so there is a lot of deep, clinical depression. You feel it in the classroom. A significant number contemplate or attempt suicide. A lot of my students purposely cut off contact with their families because it's too painful. They tell their families, including their children, to think of them as if they were dead. It's a hard place even to teach.

The guys I teach in East Jersey State Prison, a lot of them are getting out. They'll say, "Hey, I'm about to get out," and I'll say, "When?" and they'll say, "Five years." Time is relative in a prison.

Prison has the same kind of strata as in the rest of society. You have people of amazing integrity and brilliance, and you have shit bags, and people who are just going along. Prison society replicates the wider society. The difference is that some prisoners have a highly developed political conscious-ness that is usually lacking in universities like Princeton. Students in Princeton not only often come out of the elite, but want to remain part of the elite. They look at Princeton as a brand. Prisoners understand power in a way that a Prince-ton student is almost incapable of. They know the dark side of power and institutional racism. They know what our sys-tem of justice is really about. They have endured the worst of police violence. They know what poverty does to people. A conversation about power in a prison classroom begins at a much, much higher level.

*When I was a student radical at UC-Santa Cruz, the prison rights movement was on the rise, and a number of dynamic leaders like George Jackson were emerging behind bars. In fact, some fellow students and I taught classes at Soledad Prison, where Jackson was held and where he wrote the essays that made him famous,* that were collected

**in books like Soledad Brother.** *There was a sense of revolutionary ferment behind bars in those years…*
That's not true now. I visited Mumia Abu Jamal in prison—he's an old revolutionary, but he said the younger prisoners spend all their time in front of the TV. He said when he got off death row and moved to the prison at Frackville, Pennsylvania where he is now, he was walking the yard and everybody was talking about "Sam said this and Mary said that." And he thought, "Man, these people must come from the same city and know the same people." Until he found out they were all talking about TV shows.

When black radicals started entering prison in the '60s, the authorities created isolation units for them. They wanted to separate the black radicals, so their ideas couldn't spread. So someone like Ojore Lutalo, who was a member of the Black Liberation Army, spent 22 years in isolation at Trenton State Prison in New Jersey before he was released. He never committed an infraction, they just didn't want him preaching revolution, building consciousness.

*I assume your classes raise political consciousness?*
Last spring I taught a history course—*Open Veins of Latin America, Bury My Heart at Wounded Knee* and Caribbean historian C. L. R. James' *Black Jacobins*.

*Does the prison administration censor your reading list?*
They see the books. They have not censored them. I taught a drama course, we read plays by August Wilson and others. I spent four months helping them write their own play, *Caged*, which, if we get can get funded, will be performed in New York.

*So you're seeing literary talent, but not a lot of political awareness like the old days?*

The Muslims have a consciousness in terms of their own identity as African Americans. They all know Malcolm, George Jackson, Julius Lester. They're more cohesive as a community. The Muslims will never swear in class. They will do their prayers five times a day. They are tribal in the sense if someone gets shanked in the dining hall and they're not a Muslim, they won't do much—but if they are a Muslim, it's a different story.

*Speaking of Muslims, let's talk about how the Muslim population has borne the brunt of our massive security crackdown since 9/11. In the Bay Area, there's a recent case of a 22-year-old Muslim American, the son of a Silicon Valley executive, who was arrested as a suspected terrorist and held without trial for a year, for simply trying to board a flight to Turkey, where, according to his attorney, he was going to help Syrian refugees. But the government said he was going to help a rebel group fighting against the Syrian dictator Assad. Of course, the US wants to get rid of Assad too, but apparently this young man picked the wrong anti-Assad group. But the point is, it seems like he hadn't done anything illegal by the time he was arrested at the San Francisco Airport. He had committed what in the dystopian world of Philip K. Dick would be called a "pre-crime." Is that where we've come to in America, where people are being arrested and held for unlimited periods in some dark cell for thought crimes?*

Yeah, of course.

*Most people don't realize—going back to our discussion of your lawsuit against the Obama administration—that we've been living under a state of emergency in this country since 9/11, where all sorts of violations of our constitutional rights are now routinely permitted.*

No privacy, no habeas corpus, most people don't have a right to trial. In prison they arbitrarily extend your sentence for infractions.

*They can keep you inside interminably if they don't like what you're up to politically or what you're saying or even thinking...*

We have the façade of a functioning capitalist democracy, but underneath, it is a species of corporate totalitarianism. My students in the prison get this—instantly– in a way the students at Princeton did not.

*Give me an example of that.*

I gave a talk at an upper-class church in New Jersey and the people started walking out when I said that we have decapitated far more people—including children—through our drones and other aerial assaults than ISIS had ever decapitated. Say that in the prison…they get it instantly. That's a perfect example.

I was teaching [W.E.B.] DuBois, who I like, but DuBois has this notion of the "talented ten percent"—these are the elite group of African Americans who will lead the race and make a significant impact. The rest, says DuBois, can be carpenters. My class says, "Well, we aren't the talented ten." And I said, "No, let me tell you why DuBois is wrong." Those I was speaking to at that church about drones had at least a college degree, if not a graduate degree. But they couldn't hear it. They believe in the virtue of American empire.

*Against all evidence to the contrary. Just to show the deterioration in our public ethics...back in the 1970s, when the Church Committee revealed the CIA had targeted several foreign leaders for assassination, there was a public uproar and Congress took steps to impose more oversight on the CIA. But now the agency routinely assassinates people every week, including American citizens, and the only people who seem to make an issue out of it are the ACLU. The public seems vastly indifferent, even supportive of our drone killing program—and there's a collective yawn from the media when journalists like* The Intercept's *Jeremy Scahill publishes* The Drone Papers, *the leaked documents showing that most victims of these strikes in Afghanistan are innocent civilians.*

We will pay dearly for our collective complacency. This illustrates the death of civic virtue and the surrender of a demobilized and depoliticized population.

*And so, the criminality of power continues...*

And will get worse.

*It was historically important what happened in Nuremberg after World War II, where a line was drawn—and the world was told, "War crimes like this are not permissible." And the people responsible for these crimes must be held individually accountable for these crimes against humanity, even if they were acting on orders from their government. Even if they were told they were protecting their nation against ruthless enemies and "terrorists," to use a word that the Nazis also employed to enforce obedience.*

But justice was not universally dispensed after World War II. The people who committed the crimes of dropping the atomic bombs on Nagasaki and Hiroshima, or fire bombing Dresden or Tokyo, were never brought to justice.

*That's true, justice was not universal. After wars, justice belongs to the victors. But the principles of justice established at Nuremberg were vital. And our own system is incapable of this kind of moral reckoning, when it comes to our own war crimes.*

It collapsed with the pardoning of Nixon. The moment they pardoned Nixon there was no accountability left.

*I would go back earlier in my lifetime to the assassination of President Kennedy. We still don't have a true understanding of what happened in Dallas. When you can kill the leader of your country in broad daylight and then mount a sham of an investigation run by the slain president's political enemies -- including Allen Dulles, the CIA spymaster fired by JFK—then a certain rot begins to set in. I mean that was the beginning of this great questioning of authority that swept through my generation in the '60s.*

But the difference was that any complicity in the killing of Kennedy was covered up. Nixon's crimes were completely open and they were never punished.

*US war crimes in Vietnam were also widely revealed, but nobody was ever held accountable, not even for some of the most publicized atrocities, like the My Lai massacre.*

Yes, that's right. Nick Turse did a good book on that, *Kill Anything That Moves.*

*America just sleepwalks from one war, or from one assassination, to the next, with the country refusing to look deeply into these national nightmares.*

After the Vietnam War, we did look. And then, I think you are right, people weren't held accountable for the atrocities. But there was revulsion at what we did in Vietnam. America was briefly forced to ask questions about itself that it had not asked before—and we became a better nation because of that. Unfortunately, we then saw the resurrection of war's good name under Reagan, and all of that capacity to be introspective was obliterated. Now we're back to where we were.

*And the crimes of power extend to the private, sexual realm. Every so often, a sex scandal involving the rich or powerful gives the public a peek inside the corrupt sexual behavior that is allowed to flourish in parts of this privileged world. I'm thinking of men like Dominique Strauss-Kahn, the former French politician and IMF chief, or former Speaker of the House Dennis Hastert, who was one of the most powerful political figures in the US. People in the media business often hear rumors of pedophile rings and exclusive clubs and ranches where the powerful go to satisfy their most debauched desires. How extensive do you think this corruption is—and why doesn't it get investigated more?*

It is very extensive. The elites, throughout history, have used their privilege and power to turn those around them into objects they abuse for their own pleasure. Yes, it comes out once in a while, as it did with Dominique Strauss-Kahn and Dennis Hastert, but like rape on college campuses only a tiny fraction of this sexual assault is ever exposed. It does not get investigated more because the elites—and I include elitist institutions like Harvard—have the resources to buy off victims or discredit and intimidate them. Strauss-Kahn and Hastert did this. This is why Strauss-Kahn's victim dropped the case against him. Hastert spent $ 1.7 million to keep a victim silent. His abuse was only exposed because the abnormally high cash withdrawals attracted the attention of the FBI. It was widely believed when I was at the *Times* that George W. Bush had an illegitimate son. The reporters had his name. They knew the name of the mother. They knew where they lived in Texas. They had pictures—he looked a lot like Bush. But the Bush family allegedly paid off the woman to keep silent. This is so common among the elites it is taken for granted.

***Speaking of Harvard…after years of institutional cover-ups—including at some of the most prestigious universities in the country—campus rape has finally come out of the closet, thanks to the brave students who have made this a national issue. Why do you think even supposedly liberal and enlightened universities like Harvard and Berkeley have been so slow and obstructionist in their response to this problem?*** Violence against girls and women is still a taboo subject within liberal institutions that remain bastions of patriarchy and white male privilege. We have seen that the response of these colleges—as was true when my older son Thomas wrote an investigative piece for the student newspaper at Colgate on hazing and sexual assault in the fraternities—is to cover up the assaults and marginalize and demonize the victims. In Thomas' case, he was banned from writing for the school paper after an outcry from alumni and fraternity members. The abuses were never investigated by the administration, although these institutions pay lip service to all the right values. The primary concern of these institutions is always to protect their image. They will go to great lengths to do so. Given the rate at which sexual assaults and rapes appear to occur on college campuses, it is safe to say that the vast majority of the victims are never heard and the vast majority of the perpetrators are never exposed or punished.

The exploitation of girls and women, however, has been made worse with the rise of the pornified culture, a culture where violence against women is part of the sexual awakening of nearly every boy and young man. The Abu Ghraib images of prisoners being sexually humiliated and abused, for example, could have been lifted from porn films. Sexual abuse and rape is part of the wider ethic of exploitation that defines corporate capitalism. The sexualized images in porn, or from Abu Ghraib, reflect the wider racism, callousness and perversion that define our predatory, capitalist culture. It is the language of absolute control, total domination, racial stereotypes and humiliating submission. It is, in short, about reducing human beings to commodities, to objects.

Corporate culture, neoliberal ideology, imperialism and colonialism strip people of their human attributes and celebrate domination. They banish equality, tenderness, compassion and love. This is also the goal of rape. Absolute power over another, as I saw in war, expresses itself through dehumanization, violence and sexual sadism.

# XI. The Morality of Capitalism, Climate Change, Pornography, and Meat

---

*As long as we're talking about America's fundamental sins, the United States represents the highest stage of capitalism. And you clearly look at capitalism, in almost a religious way, as an evil.*

Well, of course it's evil. It's about exploitation, as Marx understood.

*Obviously I agree with you on that analysis, but is there a danger of injecting a moral fervor into politics, especially in your case, considering your religious background?*

No, the problem is we *haven't* injected a moral fervor into politics, which is why it's become immoral. If you're not willing to stand for anything, if you're constantly guided by whatever the latest opinion poll or focus group is....I mean, just watch Hillary Clinton, she's completely protean. She ran an entire campaign during the Democratic primaries that defied everything she's stood for in three decades in office...

**During the primaries, Saturday Night Live *did a sketch with their Hillary impersonator, and by the end she has morphed into a Bernie look-alike and she tells the camera, "Come on people, I'm just trying to be whatever you want me to be."***

Well that's it. And of course it's not just her. Obama was the same. I've seen real leadership. I've seen [Yitzhak] Rabin, in Israel. I saw Rabin, this old warrior, stand up and acknowledge that the occupation of the Palestinian territories was killing his country. All hell broke loose. People forget what a reviled figure he was. *That's* leadership. He had a vision and he pulled the rest of the country with him.

*Climate change is obviously a paramount issue to you, as it must be for anyone concerned about life on our planet. It normally gets framed as an environmental, political or economic issue—but more and more it strikes me as a moral issue. The energy industry officials and their hired political representatives who are primarily responsible for blocking climate change progress must not only face themselves every morning in the mirror—but their children and grandchildren too. Nobody— not even the wealthy and their heirs—is going to be entirely immune from the ravages of climate change. How do you think people like this explain themselves to their own children?*

They create a morally fragmented universe. They separate what they do in work—which they see as inevitable with or without them—from who they are as human beings. They define themselves by being a good father or mother, a good husband or wife, by acts of charity, by going to church or synagogue. They highlight acts of compassion—no matter how trivial—and use these acts as a template for their personality. Human beings, even those who commit acts of extraordinary evil, have a need to see themselves as good. They engage in extraordinary forms of self-deception to make this fiction possible. This is how the physicist who makes nuclear weapons rationalizes his or her life. This is how workers in a plant that makes napalm are able to pretend they are not responsible for the bodies of burned children.

*Already some cataclysmic geopolitical events— like the rise of ISIS and other terror groups and the refugee crises in the Middle East and Africa—have been linked to climate change. And according to Pentagon planners and others who do strategic forecasts, we can expect more and more global traumas in the future. When do you think our corporate and political systems—in the interest of preserving their own power, if nothing else—will respond to the havoc of climate change?*

The global elites will not impede the profits, or halt government subsidies, for the fossil fuel industry and the extraction industries. They will not curtail extraction. They will not impose carbon taxes. They will not limit overconsumption. They are servants of global capitalism. They will continue to siphon off trillions of dollars and direct scientific and technical expertise –expertise that should be directed toward preparing for environmental catastrophe and investing in renewable energy—to wage endless wars and consolidate corporate power. They will continue to utter empty platitudes about saving the climate while shoving new trade agreements down our throats, agreements that ignore what are anyway nonbinding climate accords. These elites will be replaced or we are doomed.

Like all civilizations careening toward collapse, we have become hostage to complex structures, and ever more intricate specialization, to exploit diminishing resources. Technocrats rule us. They are trained and indoctrinated in elite schools. They function as systems managers. They only know how to serve the system. They cannot critique it or challenge it. They are devoid of creativity or the ability to think independently. They will maintain the system at all costs. They will plunder and squander resources to serve global capitalism, even as these resources are being destroyed or exhausted. On some level they are idiots.

The systems and technologies designed to exploit these resources will eventually become useless. Economists call this the "Jevons paradox." The result is widespread systems collapse. This is where we are headed. And it will come at the end with a dizzying speed. Collapse means a severe weakening or destruction of centralized power. It means a shortage of basic amenities, including food and water. It means a violent scramble for diminishing resources. Law and order breaks down.

The Anthropocene Age—the age of humans, which has caused mass extinctions of plant and animal species and the pollution of the soil, air and oceans—is underway. I fear it is irreversible. The pace of destruction is accelerating. Sea levels are rising three times faster than predicted. The Arctic ice is vanishing at rates that were unforeseen. Even if we stop carbon emissions today—we have already reached 400 parts per million—it seems likely that carbon dioxide concentrations will continue to climb to 550 ppm. Global temperatures, even in the best of scenarios, will therefore rise for at least another century. And this assumes we actually confront this crisis today—which we show no signs of doing.

Interlocking systems will suddenly no longer be able to sustain each other. This breakdown, therefore, will be nonlinear. It will not be defined by a single event such as rising temperatures. We will see entire ecosystems and social and political institutions that sustain life—which make a complex society function—disintegrate, probably at roughly the same time. The infrastructures that distribute food, supply our energy, ensure our security, produce and transport consumer products, and maintain law and order will fray and crumble under the strain. The combined assault of soaring temperatures, submerged island states and coastal cities, mass migrations, violence, war, species extinction, monster storms, declining crop yields, droughts and famines will define much of the planet. A pervasive and ruthless security and surveillance apparatus, along with a heavily militarized police empowered to use indiscriminant lethal force, will turn industrial nations into climate fortresses to keep out refugees—we are already seeing this in Europe and along our border with Mexico—and make sure that a restive and desperate population inside these fortresses remains frightened and under control. The elites will retreat to protected compounds where they will have access to services and amenities, including food, water and medical care, denied to the rest of us. It will become the world Hobbes feared.

*Let's move on to your passionate veganism and your hard line against pornography—is that in some ways a reflection of your religious training? Is there a danger in what some regard as your politics of purity? The so-called sex-positive feminists like Susie Bright have long argued against anti-porn absolutists like the late Andrea Dworkin—they say that some forms of porn or "erotica" are liberating for men and women alike. And speaking of veganism, millions of people around the world depend on fishing, game and animal farming for their daily protein needs. Have you adopted an absolutist position on these questions?*

Let's start with porn. I'm against the commodification of human beings. Porn is one more aspect of that. I spent a lot of time reporting on the porn industry. [Ed. Note: Hedges wrote about the pornography industry in his collection, *Empire of Illusion,* and in subsequent essays in *Truthdig,* including "Pornography Is What the End of the World Looks Like."] Most of the performers, as Rachel Moran [author of *Paid For*, a memoir of her seven years in the sex trade] observes, are prostitutes. Porn is filmed prostitution. It's about being raped for a living. I started interviewing porn actresses and it was clear from the moment they started speaking that they had PTSD.

So, for me, you can't stand up against the commodification of women in a sweatshop in Bangladesh with all the physical and emotional abuse that comes with it, and not stand up against the commodification of women in the porn industry. I don't have the porn gene. It does nothing for me. I'm with Andrea Dworkin on this—I see a tremendous hypocrisy on the Left about sexual exploitation...

**But Andrea Dworkin believed that even the act of penetration was an offense against women.**

At the end of her life, but she doesn't write that in her book [*Pornography: Men Possessing Women*]. Her book on pornography is really good. She nails it. My own experience interviewing people in the industry is that they're all taking painkillers –I'm talking about the women—before they go on the set. And they're constantly going in for surgery for vaginal and anal tears. It's about violence, about eroticizing violence. It fits with a society where everybody has become an object to exploit.

The seduction of the Left when it comes to the so-called liberating aspects of porn, or the self-determination of sex workers, is bullshit. It's part of the incredible naiveté of the Left. As a war correspondent, I was around prostituted women for 20 years. War breeds prostitutes like it breeds corpses. These women were refugees. We have to remember that 98 percent of prostitutes are poor women of color who are trafficked around the world. They're trafficked because they are they are desperate. It isn't the Hollywood version of Pretty *Woman*.

**Well on a global level, this is clearly the sordid truth about the sex industry, these are women who are being ruthlessly exploited because they have no other options. But there are different zones, like the San Francisco Bay Area, where it's a different story – where certain subcultures of men and women perform on camera or onstage with each other, for their own pleasure and profit. You can say these are exhibitionistic people…**

I would argue they need a psychiatrist. Look, women in our society are hyper-sexualized and objectified. This is the context in which these kinds of events take place. Performing a sexual act in front of an audience is not conducive to intimacy and love. It feeds into the hyper-sexualization and objectification of women. How is this empowering for women and not exploitative?

**So you are fundamentally opposed to pornography as an industry of exploitation. But do you have a problem with the artistic depiction of the naked body? With erotic art?**
I don't have a problem with eroticism. Porn is inhuman and plastic.

**But you don't have a problem with the nude body as an object of beauty?**
No. I have a problem with a naked woman being fucked by 30 men in a row while being slapped and called a slut and a bitch.

**What about Japanese erotica that shows multiple partners and all that? There's a long tradition of depicting unconventional sex acts in many cultures, of course.**
Yes, porn has existed in various forms, going back to Pompeii. So has the commodification of women. So has slavery. Women in ancient cultures were usually considered property and controlled by men. This is still true. Patriarchy has been with us for thousands of years. There are traditional systems of exploitation we should get rid of.

**But Japanese erotica, for example, sometimes shows women getting pleasure too—it's not just about subjugation.**
I am not against erotica as long as women have equality and agency. Male interpretations of porn and erotica are, how-

ever, usually colored by their own perceptions and desires. The voices of women are rarely heard. Porn is about women degrading themselves physically and emotionally for men. What do women say in porn? "Fuck me, fuck me hard. I'm your whore." It's degrading. It's sick. Porn is not about sex. Porn is about masturbation.

**I understand, but I'm just trying to get you to define what your specific objection is to the visual depiction of sex acts. I mean do you object to the depiction of group sex, wild orgies, on principle—even if it looks like it's consensual, as in some of the classic porn unearthed in Pompeii or produced in imperial Japan?**

I've been in the brothels in Pompeii and Herculaneum. Girls, women and courtesans in ancient societies like Rome were often property. We haven't even mentioned the sexual exploitation of young boys. Sex is about love. It is about the capacity to mutually express physically what is emotionally present. Porn, like prostitution, is about auto-arousal, usually of a male. It celebrates male patriarchy and male domination. It is a form of misogyny. If people want to call me a purist, I don't care…I had a translator of mine in Iraq who was being pimped out as a refugee. I spent a long time looking for her and when I found her she was a psychological wreck.

**Is masturbation in the absence of porn also problematic for you?**

No. It's masturbation based on the degradation of women and violence against women that is a problem. Porn is destructive to relationships. The idea that I'm a purist or I don't like sex is ridiculous. And the Left is guilty of promulgating this bullshit. The whole defense of the porn industry shows how out of touch the Left is with the exploitation of the underclass, especially girls and women.

I've done reporting on this, I wrote a piece called "Recalled to Life" about a former heroin addict and prostitute in Camden. I did a piece on Rachel Moran, who was a prostituted woman in Ireland for many years—in addition to all the women I witnessed in war zones for many years. People don't want to be treated like a piece of meat. They want to be treated like a human being. They want and deserve to be loved and treated with dignity. My objection to porn, like prostitution, is that girls and women are dehumanized and objectified. They are drained of their humanity. That's it.

### Do you have the same critique of the gay porn industry, where the power dynamics involving the male performers seem somewhat different?

The gay culture has tops and bottoms, those who are hyper-masculine and those who are hyper-feminine. I suspect the same degradation of the "effeminate" man goes on. It is also, I suspect, mostly about masturbation. But this is not something I know much about.

### All right, jumping to veganism…by the way, did we just eat cheese in this flatbread? [At this point, the conversation has moved to a tavern in Princeton serving happy-hour snacks.] Are you a strict vegan?

There might have been cheese. I usually order it without cheese. I am not always as diligent as my wife. I switched to veganism largely for environmental reasons. I buy the species-ism argument, but what tipped the balance for me was the destructive force of the animal-based agriculture industry in terms of global warming.

## *Industrial farming?*

All this was made clear to me in the documentary Cowspiracy. It was a piece of the corporate assault I had missed, in part because of the blackout of reporting imposed by the industry. The animal agriculture is responsible for more greenhouse gas emissions than all the cars, trucks, trains, ships and planes combined. Livestock, along with their waste and flatulence, account for at least 32,000 million tons of carbon dioxide ($CO_2$) per year, or 51 percent of all worldwide greenhouse gas emissions. Livestock causes 65 percent of all emissions of nitrous oxide. Nitrous oxide is a greenhouse gas 296 times more destructive than carbon dioxide. Crops grown for livestock feed consume 56 percent of the water used in the United States. Eighty percent of the world's soy crop is fed to animals and the rain forests are being destroyed – 91 percent in the Amazon—so soy for animals can be grown on cleared lands. Land devoted exclusively to raising livestock now represents 45 percent of the earth's land mass. In the United States 70 percent of the grain we grow goes to feed livestock raised for consumption, this as six million children a year died across the globe from starvation.

The natural resources used to produce animal products cannot be justified in a time of scarcity and climate change. It takes 1,000 gallons of water to produce one gallon of milk. We are destroying the lungs of the earth to feed the profits of the animal agriculture industry. It is not a huge adjustment in our eating habits to halt our complicity in this assault.

## *But you've also written that all life is sacred, so you do have a moral component to your veganism.*

Yes, that's true. I couldn't eat meat after Sarajevo. I saw bodies that looked like butchered meat. I stopped eating meat a long time ago. I did eat fish.

***Even though you embrace the all life is sacred argument?***
I stopped eating fish when I became a vegan.

***Would you have an objection to a local family farm that produces cheese?***
Local farms usually do not treat animals much better than industrial farms. And I won't eat any product that involves torturing or killing an animal. We shouldn't eat cheese anyway because of the cholesterol, saturated fat and high levels of sodium.

***What about your kids?***
My kids are vegan. Children instinctively understand that we should not kill or harm animals if there is no need to do so.

***Can you actually slaughter the animal that you eat – that's the ultimate test isn't it? When I was starting out in journalism, I couldn't eat meat after hanging out in a slaughterhouse, where I was writing about the workers on the killing floor. But I could milk a cow.***
Right, I could milk a cow…in fact, I *have* milked a cow. Cows on most farms, however, are milked by machines. They are physically abused, repeatedly impregnated with sperm guns while being constrained on rape racks, kept in a constant state of lactation and usually have their calves taken from them at birth and killed for veal. As soon as the diary cows cannot produce enough milk to be profitable, usually after four to five years, they are slaughtered. They have a natural lifespan of about 25 years. It is not a pretty industry.

# XII. Maintaining Your Humanity Even While Cruelty Reigns

*Well, this all comes back to what we we've been talking a lot about—how to lead a moral life, which is to say, not one dictated by organized religion, but by your own internal compass, as imperfect as that might be...*

I have a friend named Lola Mozes who survived Auschwitz. Her parents, both of whom were eventually killed, protected Lola and her brother even in the most hellish of circumstances. Lola's father was killed in the ghetto with her brother. Lola and her mother ended up in Auschwitz. They survived by taking care of each other. They stayed together until the final days of the war, when the Nazis forced the prisoners on the death march. The march was too much for Lola's mother. She collapsed on the side of the road. An SS officer pulled out his pistol to shoot her. Lola—a 14-year-old girl—ran up and put her arms out in front of the SS officer and said, "You have a mother."

*And she saves her mother's life?*

No. He executes her mother. But until the very end, the mother and daughter—even in the midst of this horror—cling to their love and humanity.

*Was this published in* **Truthdig?**

Yes. It was about 4,000 words.

*What kind of response did you get from readers?*

I don't know. I wrote it for myself. I wrote it for Lola. I wrote it for her parents. Her parents, on one level, won the war. They saved their daughter from hate. The love they gave to her she passed on to her own children and grandchildren. A love this fierce is eternal.

***Do you think the meek of the earth are always doomed to be victims? Going back to our discussion of revolution, it seems that the idealists always get quickly eliminated when revolutions turn violent.***

Idealists are eliminated when revolutions turn violent. I'd be doomed in a violent revolution. Che Guevara and Lenin understood that iron-fisted actions are necessary to consolidate power. They had only one single-minded goal. I have another goal, to be a moral being. This puts me at a severe disadvantage. Julien Benda in *The Treason of the Intellectuals* says we have two options in life. We can serve justice and truth or privilege and power. The more we make compromises with those who serve privilege and power, the more we diminish our capacity for justice and truth. Better, as an intellectual or an artist, to always be a heretic.

*Well, in the case of Fidel and Che, they learned from the fate of Jacobo Arbenz and his peaceful, democratic revolution. Che was in Guatemala in 1954, at the time of the CIA-led military coup against Arbenz—he urged Arbenz to arm the peasants and fight back. But Arbenz didn't—he stepped down and went into exile. And the CIA-backed military government that replaced Arbenz turned Guatemala into the bloody killing fields that he was trying to avoid by peacefully stepping aside.*

That's true. Che learned that the US would stop at nothing. He was not wrong in his assessment.

*And, as a result, the Cuban revolution survived the CIA's Bay of Pigs invasion and countless CIA assassination attempts against Castro. The lesson of Cuba does seem to be that only revolutionaries with iron resolve survive the inevitable plots and military counter assaults by imperial forces.*

Yes. This is true. I would have ended up like Carlos Franqui if I were Cuban—he was the Cuban writer and early supporter of the revolution, who broke with Castro and went into exile in Italy.

*At least Castro let Franqui go and live his life in peace.*

That would not have been true under Lenin. He got rid of all his intellectuals. At first he deported them, then he executed them.

*So there is generally a psychopathology of power – and the ruthless leaders are the ones who inevitably win out in these revolutionary situations? I mean psychopaths usually win…*

As soon as a revolution becomes violent, people like me are doomed. Those who have a penchant for violence, an ability for ruthlessness, take over the resistance. After the revolution, because they have the guns, they have control. That's why I'm so strongly against violence.

Yet, the fate of a revolution is not solely in the revolutionaries' control. It's the dominant power system that determines the response. As the power system uses harsher and harsher forms of control in order to maintain power, it inevitably provokes counter violence. I don't blame it on the revolutionaries. The state ultimately determines the configurations of rebellion. But violence, even in a supposedly just cause, is always tragic.

Shutting down the Occupy encampments wasn't a rational response by the state. A rational response would have been to declare a moratorium on foreclosures and bank repossessions, institute a massive jobs program targeted especially at people under age 25, forgive all student debt and create a universal heath care system…*that* would have been rational. That would have gone a long way to blunting the anger and the rage that we are now seeing rise as proto-fascism in this society. The fact that the state was so myopic, that it couldn't respond rationally, is frightening. You shut down a movement like that, which was peaceful and frankly not that radical, and what comes next? Those who make peaceful revolution impossible, as John F. Kennedy said, make violent revolution inevitable.

*Of course, there are dramatic, but peaceful ways that you can confront the violence of the state. In San Francisco right now, a group of hunger strikers—including a rapper named Equipto and his 66-year-old mother Maria Cristina Gutierrez who happen to be my next-door neighbors—are engaged in a hunger strike to protest the wave of police violence against the poor, black and brown in this supposedly "liberated" city. There are obvious concerns for people who put their health on the line like this. Do you think this kind of life-threatening activism is justified in America today?*

Yes, because it dramatizes the abuse and pressures the authorities to respond. There are moments when we have to risk our lives. I had to accept this as a war correspondent. If I was not in Sarajevo during the siege, where four to five people were being killed a day and about a dozen wounded, the story would not get out. Hunger strikes have long been a tool used by the oppressed. Mahatma Gandhi carried out 17 hunger strikes or fasts, one lasting 21 days. British suffragists carried out hunger strikes. Chinese students in Tiananmen Square carried out hunger strikes. Tibetan monks carried out public fasts outside the United Nations.

Guantanamo Bay, our version of Devil's Island, has been beset since 2002 with a series of hunger strikes, often involving as much as a third of the prison. This has led to the ghoulish procedures of forced feeding. California's Pelican Bay State Prison carried out a 60-day hunger strike two years ago to protest the conditions in the prison's "security housing unit" or SHU. Cornel West, myself and many others across the country joined the hunger strikers in Pelican Bay for a day to express our solidarity.

Hunger strikes are one of the few effective tools of protest for prisoners. Andrei Sakharov, Nelson Mandela and Bobby Sands of the Irish Republican Army all led hunger strikes. Sands, of course, starved himself to death in an Irish prison. His death ignited worldwide outrage, including riots in Ireland. The propaganda value of a martyr's funeral is immense, as Sands understood.

Hunger strikes, if well publicized and carried out skillfully, are a powerful tool to raise consciousness and mobilize resistance. They are extreme forms of rebellion, but sometimes they are the only method left to get the outside world to listen to the cries of the oppressed. Once we learn how to die – which as Cornel West points out means freeing ourselves from fear along with psychic and psychological bondage—we can learn how to live.

*Speaking of non-violent resistance to the state, let's talk about Chelsea Manning, Julian Assange and Edward Snowden. To me, these are three central figures of our lives, heroes who sacrificed themselves for the good of us all.*

They did, completely.

*They were like the old biblical prophets who were trying to wake us up and warn us about the gathering darkness. But for most people, don't you think their stories are cautionary tales, since they now reside, respectively, in a military dungeon, under house arrest in a London embassy, and in exile in a country where he would prefer not to live in. So... are these cautionary tales or inspirational ones?*

Inspirational. Throughout history when you rise up, as these three people did, to speak truth—not a truth to power, because power knows what it does—but a truth about power, you're almost always crushed. That's a fact of history. Most rebels don't go on to wonderful careers—whether you are Toussaint Louverture, leading the only successful slave revolt in human history in Haiti, or Che. That's the sublime madness we talked about. The strength of real revolutionaries is that they understand this. There's a kind of pathos and power about these rebels. They know they are probably doomed, yet they act anyway. Hannah Arendt says the only morally reliable people are not those who say "this is wrong" or "this should not to be done" but those who say "I can't."

This reminds me of something that happened with my students in prison. I had to fly to Montana to give a speech. I was in my hotel room in Montana. I got a phone call: "This is the Department of Corrections' Special Investigations Division of the State of New Jersey. Do you know your students just led a sit-down strike in our prison? We think you might be behind it. Your prison credential has been revoked until you come in and see us."

These prisoners rose up, inside the prison on the day they had no class. The organized a non-violent strike. And they knew what would happen. They knew there would be harsh retribution—cells searched, interrogations, shipping the leaders to another prison and putting them in solitary, all of which happened.

### What were they striking for?
A few issues, but the big one was that the prison had banned what are called "stingers," small hot water coils that allow prisoners to heat up coffee and tea and noodle soup in their cells.

### Basic amenities of prison life.
Yes, but vital given the slop served in the mess hall. It was the only way they could heat food and drinks they bought in the commissary. I had to go in for an interrogation.

### *What did they ask you?*

I wasn't behind the strike. I knew nothing about it, The students wouldn't have been stupid enough to involve me. I told the truth. I went back to the prison classroom after being interrogated. When I walked into the classroom, my students were in shock. They could hardly speak. In a prison you have so little, you have nothing really. You have movement in the yard, you have your job, you have the ability to take a class. But at the whim of a guard, it can all be taken away. They can make you spend 23 hours a day in your cell.

### *And, like you say, they can ship you to another prison, many miles away. Have you lost track of the prisoners who were transferred?*

I know where they are. I am not allowed to contact students outside of the classroom. They monitor contacts closely.

Prison often takes people who have suffered trauma and makes them worse. But some people, I do not know how, rise above it. They achieve an incredible dignity. Nelson Mandela walked out of prison like this. I know a few prisoners who have acquired in prison great wisdom, serenity and integrity. They are some of the most impressive people I have ever met.

### *They're almost more than human...you know the Buddhist concept of bodhisattvas, holy beings who lift us all higher.*

They have the quality of a bodhisattva. I did a radio show with a man named Earl Amin who had been 34 years in prison. He'd been a Black Panther in Newark. He had been entrapped by an informant after discussing the possibility of robbing a bank. He never robbed a bank. He never had a weapon. He never committed a crime. This was during the war on black radicals. They imprisoned him for 34 years for a robbery he never committed. Earl and I were on a radio show together after he finally got out. He talked about what it was like to be inside for most of his life, how he went to the law library and wrote the divorce papers for his wife. He finally gets out, he's 65, he has no social security. He's pouring cement in Newark two days a week to live…

## *He keeps on keeping on…*

As he's telling his story on radio, I'm sitting next to him and I'm getting more and more heated. Later, my wife, who listened to the show, says to me, "Who was in prison, you or Earl?" But there's a perfect example of a man who does indeed have this Buddha-like ability. This serenity, I've seen that in prison.

I had a student in my history class who was arrested at age 14 for a murder I don't believe he committed. He had lived on the streets after this stepfather beat his mother to death in front of him. He held his mother's head as she died. He was tried as an adult. He's not eligible to go before a parole board until he's 70. He was my only A-plus student. He waited until everyone left the last class. He says, "I know I will probably die in this prison. But I work as hard as I do so that one day I can be a teacher like you." That's why I do what I do. That's why I teach in a prison. And that's why I have hope.